DARE TO THRIVE

Lessons Learned from a Trauma Survivor

GREG LINKOWSKI, MD

SILVERSMITH
PRESS

Published by Silversmith Press–Houston, Texas
www.silversmithpress.com

Copyright © 2025 Greg Linkowski

All rights reserved.

This book, or parts thereof, may not be reproduced in any form or by any means without written permission from the author, except for brief passages for purposes of reviews. For more information, contact the publisher at office@publishandgo.com.

The views and opinions expressed herein belong to the author and do not necessarily represent those of the publisher.

ISBN 978-1-961093-92-8 (Softcover Book)
ISBN 978-1-961093-93-5 (eBook)

CONTENTS

Foreword vii

Chapter 1. The Sound that Silenced the Family 1
Chapter 2. My Turbulent and Triumphant Teen Years 11
Chapter 3. Discovering My Dad 22
Chapter 4. Bonding Through Fishing
    (If There's Water...) 32
Chapter 5. The Legend of Mother Teresa
    (no, not that one) 38
Chapter 6. We've Been Working on the Railroad 46
Chapter 7. California Dreamin' 52
Chapter 8. The Valley of the Shadow of...Hell? 62
Chapter 9. Radiology, Residency, and Fellowship 67
Chapter 10. Love and Marriage–A Look
    at Our Love Story 75
Chapter 11. All That Glitters 83
Chapter 12. Changing Jobs and Changing Diapers 89

Chapter 13. David and the Early Years.................................... 93
Chapter 14. "Lord, We Need a Miracle"................................ 101
Chapter 15. Sammy the Hammy... 115
Chapter 16. Grin and Bear It...My Early Retirement............ 123
Chapter 17. My Second Act 130
Chapter 18. Dashed Dreams of Happily-Ever-After 147
Chapter 19. My Accordian Life.. 151
Chapter 20. Loss, Lessons Learned, and Legacy.................. 156

*To God and my precious family:
Where would I be without you?*

FOREWORD

I met the Linkowski family 30 years ago when they showed up in my church one Sunday morning. The Downtown Church was a small, inner-city church in Fresno, California. I did not know at the time how meeting Greg, his wife, Lynn, and their three children—especially their middle child David—would forever change my life and how I view disabled children and their place in the local church.

I asked them how they learned about our church. Lynn said that a close friend and prayer partner told her about our church and how we would be accepting and loving toward them, especially their son, David. Little David suffered with a terrible seizure disorder, developmental delays, and multiple other medical problems. David could not control his oratorical outbursts. When he get loud while I was preaching, I would say, "Okay, I got one Amen from little David, who is going to give me a second Amen?"

I was blessed to have the Linkowski family in my church, but I was doubly blessed to have little David in my life. Greg and Lynn allowed me to participate in a number of David's medical case reviews that were conducted by medical doctors, social workers, rehab specialists, nurses, etc. I would hear one negative report after another such as, "David won't be able to recognize people like you and I do." But in church, I would notice David's eyes following me from one end of the stage to the other. The medical staff would say, "David will never be able to see clearly." Then, a few Sundays later he would show up in church with glasses. In these case reviews, I would hear how David would have to be fed through a feeding tube. Then I would see him eating and swallowing on his own. I called these moments "God's Mini Miracles." When little David wasn't in pain or discomfort, he always had a smile on his face; and over time he became known as the *Welcoming Ambassador for The Downtown Church.*

Greg and Lynn would often tell of the impact David had on the lives of those who were fortunate enough to come across his path. But it wasn't until that day in October 2002 when I officiated David's memorial service that I understood just how great of an impact he actually had on the lives of so many people—from the Mayor of Fresno, corporate CEO's, blue collar workers, to the numerous medical professionals that served David during his 10-year journey; as well as the individuals who showed up from a number of other churches, and most of all, the Linkowski family themselves.

But this is a story that goes beyond David's life. This is a story about survival, overcoming those dark places in our lives, personal failures, and receiving God's grace. This is a story of faith, hope, and divine appointments. This is a story about preserving legacy long after we have left this world, and hearing God say, "Well done, thou good and faithful servant, receive your eternal reward my son, my daughter (Matthew 25:21)." Reading this book will give you a sense of hope and a reassurance of Romans 8:28, "And we know that all things work together for good to them that love God, to them who are the called according to His Purpose." How honored I have been to take this journey with Greg and his family, and now this journey of **hope** awaits you.

Doug Lanier
Senior Pastor Emeritus
Fresno, CA

CHAPTER 1
THE SOUND THAT SILENCED THE FAMILY

"I'm going upstairs to kill myself." As a 13-year-old boy, I could barely process what I had heard, especially after the gunshot buried into the kitchen floor had already shaken the house. Here I was in the living room, along with my brother and sister, standing on that brown shag carpet by the gold-colored couch covered in plastic. Knickknacks were on the built-in white shelves, along with our family photos. I was shaking with pure fright! It felt like the dark wood panels on the walls were closing in to crush all of us. This was a living nightmare being played out in real time.

Suddenly, a man staggered past me; that drunken man was my dad! Before the gunshot, mom and dad had been fighting yet again, but now we were all filled with shock and terror. He slowly began to climb the stairs waving the gun in the air. Without a word to each other, all four of us instinctively charged him as if we were warriors who had trained for this. We wrestled him to the ground

CHAPTER 1

as I wrenched that loaded gun out of his right hand. Had we not, a few short seconds later, a precious life would have been lost, and my dad would be another statistic. That scene has been replayed and revisited in my mind, mostly on an unconscious level, hundreds of times over the years.

From that point, our family had a secret that could never be talked about. I don't remember any of us saying a word about what happened for the rest of the day. I do remember that mom called the police. The two police officers who came were very kind and escorted Dad down to their squad car and off they went. I found out later that he had spent the night at the police station, and they kindly brought him to my grandmother's home for a couple of days. That night I laid awake in bed, afraid to go to sleep. Finally, I cried myself to sleep, but the night was spent tossing and turning in tumultuous and restless sleep. While Dad was gone, my brother fearlessly went down into that scary cellar and confiscated all of Dad's firearms and ammunition. Dad finally returned home appearing sedate and contrite. Our family life went on and we all pretended that nothing bad had ever really happened. Somehow a new elephant appeared in the room and things were destined to become more chaotic and difficult as the years progressed.

The Dream of My Birth

My very earliest memory came in the form of a dream when I was 40 years old. I remember that dream as if it was yesterday. I was walking along in this dark tunnel in a cave. A young couple passed by going in the opposite direction, and we all said hello. Alongside them was a small mixed breed dog that looked exactly like our family dog who was named Quimby. I struggled to get through the opening in the cave, only to be hampered by these green garden hoses, crisscrossed over each other, blocking the exit. Then I remember two giant hands reaching in, and pulling me out. I am convinced that this dream was a metaphor for my difficult birth, where forceps had to be used to deliver me.

We Did Christmas Right

Things weren't always this crazy. I can recall my early childhood which had some wonderful memories. Far and away my favorite time of the year was Christmas. There was always a feeling of joy and anticipation in our home before the big day. I especially loved decorating the tree and listening to Christmas music. When I was an altar boy, our family would usually go to midnight mass on

CHAPTER 1

Christmas Eve. We all were so excited about Christmas Day that it was hard to sleep at all. We kids would wake up before sunrise but had to remain in bed until mom and dad lit up the tree.

We were all excited as we opened all our presents. I remember us honoring each other by taking the time for each of us to open one present at a time, and we would take turns in a very orderly and loving fashion. We each were so kind, caring, and loving to each other. Looking back on that, how I wish that could have been a template for how we behaved with one another the rest of the year.

Every Christmas afternoon we had extended family celebrations, hosted by my mother's side of the family. Early on, Grandma hosted the party at her small row house. My favorite uncle brought a long bright, red woolen sock full of coins, including silver dollars, 50-cent pieces, and other coins. Even with so many cousins, each of us got our turn to put our hand deep into the bottom of the sock and pull out as many coins as we could hold. The trick to pulling out as many coins as possible was to scoop the coins and cradle them in your hand, then pull out carefully because the sock narrowed in its mid portion. Usually we lost some, even most, of the coins, however, nobody really cared. It was just magical fun. And it was a delight to have the vast spread of food, especially

Polish favorites along with desserts. I would bring along my accordion and play some Christmas songs where most everyone sang.

Outdoor Times Were Great

Winter fun included sleigh rides, snow forts, and snowball fights. There were tons of kids in my neighborhood, so we chose teams and would even take prisoners from the opposite team. However, the prisoners and our dungeons were safe from getting hit from the snowballs in in the sheltered and protected fort. Boy, did we have fun!

During the summer we squealed with joy while being sprayed with water hoses in the backyard and running through the sprinklers. We also enjoyed going to various lakes and public pools and parks. Our neighbors had pools and going in them was a special treat. Some summer nights we would be visited by a neighbor boy who dressed up and pretended to be Zorro. He would run up and down the street with a small stick and flash the letter Z. Early on, we actually believed he was the real Zorro just like on the TV show.

My brothers and I were all fire bugs. I learned a lesson one day that was seared into my memory. About ten of us children were playing in a vacant lot adjacent to

CHAPTER 1

other homes in the neighborhood. We had a small fire going, and I asked one of the older boys if a small strand of hay placed into the fire could start another fire if I moved that straw to another location. He assured me that could not happen, so of course I tried it. A few moments later nearly the whole lot caught fire, almost causing a neighbor to call the fire department. Fortunately, we were all able to extinguish it without any damage to any of the homes. I learned a valuable lesson about how dangerous fire can be.

Summertime Was Greater

At least once during the summer, Dad would pile in as many neighborhood kids as could fit into the old '54 Chevy station wagon and head out to Playland. While I can't remember exactly, I know kids were crammed into all the seats, on the floor, and probably in the trunk. I think there were about ten of us give or take a couple. Although money was tight, Dad would treat all of us to as many rides, cotton candy, and hot dogs that we could take in until the money ran out. At least once during the summer, Dad would take all of us kids for about a week to our aunt and uncle's home up in Kingston, New York. They lived on a farm and had children near our age. We got to experience country living. We helped feed the chickens and rode horses. We went shooting in the shale pit, as well as going swimming in the creek down the road. We also enjoyed exploring and fishing and all sorts of games and would play from dawn until dusk.

As we got a bit older, Dad would take us for a week-long vacation up to a town called Hague on the northern part of beautiful Lake George. The memories of swimming, fishing, going to Fort Ticonderoga, visiting the papermill, and getting extra special treatment from Dad were priceless.

The Role of Eldest

There were some darker memories. My older sister developed a serious infection when I was around five or six. Shortly afterwards it seemed as though I was ordained to become like the oldest child in the family. Unfortunately, I was favored more by mom and resented more by dad. Family life gradually became more dysfunctional and chaotic. My brothers and I all engaged in sibling rivalry, and I would challenge each of them to wrestling matches; lose or win, it didn't really seem to matter all that much. Heck, I didn't know any better, we were just kids! My role in the family was to excel in school, and to this day I remain

CHAPTER 1

grateful for this escape route enabling me to become a medical doctor. Somehow, I became the symbol of the healthy one in my family, which was very hard to imagine considering how dysfunctional a unit my family was. As a youngster, I got hold of a book called *The Making of a Psychiatrist*, and for the longest time, I really believed with all my heart that that was to be my destiny.

Fast forward to medical school and my clinical clerkship in psychiatry. One of the inpatients on the psychiatric ward committed suicide one weekend while in the facility. My spirit was crushed and I realized there was no way I could then or ever become a psychiatrist. Of course, I would understand later that the underlying reason for wanting to become a psychiatrist was to be able to cure my family. None of these things ever happened. My siblings chose other paths out of the darkness, but we all paid the price of exit. Some of us probably paid a heavier price than others. As we've grown older, through the grace of God, we have become even closer as we share traveling the path of life with one another.

On Being Catholic

During the 50s and 60s, my mom and dad were just like many other parents in our neighborhood. If you were white and Catholic, you had a one-way ticket to heaven that was bought and paid for. It didn't seem to matter much how you lived during the week as long as you went to church on Sunday. You could essentially live like the devil for most of the week, then go to confession, and you were all cleansed. If you weren't Catholic, good luck.

To help make ends meet, Mom went back to work as an executive secretary when I was in grade school. That came with pros and cons. Because she was working, I got to experience care from other adults and families, which I believe that provided a richer upbringing. Then there were those times when we were left to our own devices and would get into mischief.

My early education was in public school from kindergarten through second grade. One of the only memories I have from first grade was being in love with my teacher, who was just adorable. Then came private Catholic school, mostly staffed by Dominican nuns. Those were the good old days in the 60s, when hitting was fitting. They were a diverse bunch. Some were saint-like while others had a mean streak a mile wide. One of the worst things that I witnessed was when one of the students was misbehaving during music class. The nun in charge marched over to him, and clapped both sides of his head simultaneously, like cymbals. I'm sure his ears were ringing.

CHAPTER 1

Still Positive After All These Years

All in all, I am grateful to have lived my childhood. Having lived through the composite of good and enjoyable experiences, combined with the painful traumatic ones, has given me a deeper understanding of life itself. My goal is to bring a message of hope and encouragement and present the notion of never giving up despite whatever terrible experiences life might throw at you. I believe we are all here to learn, and God never gives us more than we can handle. (My rationale is that God must love me an awful lot, ha ha!) We each face challenges, problems, and opportunities on our paths in life. The important thing is how we respond and react to those events and hopefully maintain as positive an attitude as we can as we move forward.

CHAPTER 2
MY TURBULENT AND TRIUMPHANT TEEN YEARS

Growing up in Yonkers, NY was, well, let's just say colorful. Yonkers used to be called the city of gracious living, and indeed was the fabled home for the movie and musical *Hello Dolly!*. Being the oldest boy in my family, I felt it was my job to keep my two younger brothers in line. I would take both of them on in wrestling matches, but it didn't seem to matter to any of us who won. We would finish the match then go on with our day.

The "Fun" in Dysfunction

Anarchy ruled in my family. On a scale from 1 to 10, my family's degree of dysfunction was an 11! We actually put the fun in dysfunction; and malfunction as time went on. Mom and Dad predominantly communicated with each other by bickering and arguing. I never remember seeing them hugging each other, holding hands, or ever saying

CHAPTER 2

I love you. A typical day might start out OK, but at any moment the bell would ring, and they would each come out swinging. That was negative relationship training.

The Darker Side of Dysfunction

I've attempted to unpack my understanding of what led to Dad's attempted suicide. Things in my family really began to go sideways when I was around age nine or ten. Over the years I have strived to understand him better, even after he had passed, and have devoted a later chapter to my dad. I am certain that he acquired PTSD (post-traumatic stress disorder) from his World War II experiences in combat while serving in the Navy. Like most other men and women who served in World War II, he never got the kind of care and treatment that he needed. Dad began drinking on a progressively heavier level on weekends. Overtime this was supplemented with scotch, gin, vodka, or whiskey; pretty much whatever he could get his hands on. Dad would carefully hide small flasks filled with alcohol in key locations, particularly at the entrance to the cellar and down in the basement. He would drink when pretending to go down there to work on various projects. I often had a feeling of impending doom when I knew Dad was down in the cellar.

Before Dad went into recovery, we would hunt for his flasks and larger bottles of alcohol and pour them out in the sink. That was a miserable failure. Now I know that he drank to numb his pain, both from the war and in his marriage. Before his actual suicide attempt, he talked about killing himself a number of times.

Both Mom and Dad had equal roles to play in our family dysfunction. Mom would often tell us that the only reason she was staying in our home was because of us kids. This of course led to a lot of feelings of guilt; that somehow we were responsible for our parents' unhappiness. My own PTSD has been replayed in countless nightmares where I would see visions of Satan and other scary ghosts down in that dark forbidden cellar. In those dreams I would often call on God to banish those devils, and indeed He did!

An Early Start to Drink

By the age of 13 or 14, my buddies and I began drinking beer, wine, and whatever hard liquor we could get our hands on over the weekends. Sometimes we would go camping, but that was mainly an excuse to bring along a case of beer. We would drink the whole case. Sometimes we would chug the can of beer by punching a hole in the bottom of the can with a can opener, hold it up to our

CHAPTER 2

mouths, and then open the flip top. Why that way you could guzzle a whole can in about two or three seconds. There was an old Schaefer beer commercial set to music, "Schaefer is the one beer to have, when you're having more than one." We always abided by that commercial. We also smoked pot on occasion. To this day I am grateful that my drug experimentation went no further than that.

An Early Start to Work

When I turned 12 years old, I got my first paper route. I thoroughly enjoyed delivering papers to the homes in a neighborhood adjacent to where we lived. Once a week I would ring the doorbell or knock on the door and call out, "Paper boy, collecting." I later inherited the easiest paper route ever—an entire eight-floor apartment building about three blocks from my house. My new endeavor took me only 30 minutes to deliver all the papers. The money just rolled in every week. I was starting to feel all grown up.

One summer, when I was 15, I saw an ad in the newspaper for a telephone operator for a local taxi company. During the job interview, the boss looked me in the eye and asked me my age. I simply stretched the truth by a few months and told him I was 16. At that time in my life

MY TURBULENT AND TRIUMPHANT TEEN YEARS

I probably looked like I was 13 or 14, and while I'm certain he knew the truth, he hired me anyway. At this night job, I sat at a long table with a row of telephones attached to the wall, each one with a dome-shaped light on top. When the phone rang, the light would start blinking. I had so much fun on this job and loved it even more when two or three phones rang simultaneously. I believe I was so used to living in chaos that the job came like second nature to me.

I turned 16 in 1970 and got a part time job as the clerk/manager at the neighborhood Italian delicatessen. Walking into the deli, the first thing that captured your attention was a couple of huge whole provolone cheeses hanging on giant hooks. Aluminum foil was placed under them because these cheeses would drip oil. White shirts were mandatory attire at work. I fondly remember returning home smelling like cheese, reminiscent of the movie Elf, when Buddy turns to the fake Santa and says, "You smell like beef and cheese!"

I learned a lot about dealing with people, the owners, my coworkers, and the public in general. I'll never forget one day when an elderly Italian man ordered a pound of Swiss cheese. I had to start slicing a new cheese. It takes several slices to arrive at the Swiss cheese holes. He looked at the cheese on the scale and says in broken English, "That's a not a Swiss a cheese. Where are the holes?" My wise crack response leaped out of my mouth, and I responded, "Yes, it is Swiss cheese. Do you want me to poke a few holes in it for you?" I have to thank mom for my quick wit and keen sense of humor. I can't tell you what a joy it was for me to work there for a total of six years.

God is Watching

My honesty and integrity prevailed in all the store's financial transactions, and I vowed to never steal. That is until one day when I broke that vow. I gave a few pounds of cold cuts to my brother and charged him for one pound. I openly admit I did this a few more times until my conscience kicked in and I stopped that behavior. That darker side of myself plagued me for a number of years afterwards. After bringing this up in my therapy and pondering what to do, I hand wrote a letter of apology to my former boss and enclosed a check and asked for forgiveness. I'll never know if he was still alive or if the check was cashed but I finally forgave myself for this transgression. I am grateful to serve a God who not only forgives our sins at our requests but forgets them as well. That gives me hope for the future, here and eternally. Over the years I have discovered that walking in forgiveness is so important.

These days I am much more willing to ask for forgiveness and keep moving on. A valuable lesson is to be honest and forthright. God is always watching, even if nobody else is.

Early School Days

I attended Catholic grade school and became an altar boy. This was back in the good old days when the mass was still in Latin. I learned the Confiteor in Latin, when at the time I hardly knew the English translation. One of the priests was sometimes especially mean at mass. If either of the altar boys didn't recite that prayer loud enough, he would stop the mass, embarrass us, and make us repeat the prayer, only louder. That made me wonder what this man was doing in the priesthood. Then there was the jolly old Monsignor of our parish who, in my opinion, was a prince of a guy. He would usually hand out our report cards and I always looked forward to it because I did well academically. He always mentioned how our family was always smiling (well, at least we were on the outside). I wound up getting the religion award when we graduated eighth grade. I narrowly missed the high school scholarship award that went to the student with the highest GPA; however, the fellow who received it was also a friend of mine and deserved that award.

CHAPTER 2

Academics, Athletics, and Girls

Catholic high school followed. I was especially fond of learning Spanish. My first teacher was a Christian brother, followed later by a lovely Spanish lady. I developed a keen interest in biology as well.

Apart from academics, I was very shy in high school. I briefly dated a couple of girls because I knew that's what people my own age were supposed to do, yet I was never really that interested. In retrospect, although I was very shy at that time, I was well liked and was even voted most friendly of the boys in my class. My friends and I would go to some of the high school dances that were held once a month. We would often drink alcohol beforehand to get high and slip in undetected. The nuns, brothers, and priests would roam through the room while we were dancing, and say, "Make room for the Holy Spirit." As a senior, I got up the courage to ask a beautiful, tall blonde girl to go to the senior prom with me and she graciously accepted. She wore a low-cut prom dress, making me the envy of several of the other boys in my class. We even got to go water skiing on Long Island Sound the following day, making prom a very memorable experience.

For the first two years of high school, the boys and girls had separate classes. One day a couple of boys staged a pretend fight in front of one of the Christian brothers. The only person who didn't know it was a pretend fight was the brother, and it was quite hilarious. One of the funniest memories was our geometry teacher, who told us there were more horse's asses in this world than there are horses. Another brother, who was pretty surly, invited you to have tea-time with him at 4 PM if you misbehaved. Yet another brother would tell the disobedient student, "I'll knock you from here to there and back again." These are a few examples of the funny stuff I experienced.

I dabbled in sports in high school. I played intramural bowling for a couple of years, then during my senior year, ice hockey was introduced at our school. I remember playing hockey all hours of the night and early mornings at age 17 or 18. I, along with one of my brothers and my cousin would usually play offense. I even had a short stint on the varsity baseball team, but I really was never cut out to be a superior athlete. That role had been taken by my youngest brother, an athlete to this day.

Rough Start to Kick Start

Over time, I still imagined myself becoming a psychiatrist. I applied to and was accepted at Manhattan College,

CHAPTER 2

a Catholic college in the Bronx. I started my freshman year way too cocky. I had mistakenly convinced myself that I could handle a full load of pre-med courses and work 30 hours a week at the deli. However, general chemistry proved me wrong. I wound up earning a C grade both semesters. Naysayers would have said to give up my dream of becoming a doctor. But then I heard through the grapevine about this professor of comparative vertebrate and mammalian anatomy. This man was a small Italian fireball. Legend had it that if you got an A in his courses, you were well on your way to becoming a doctor or a dentist. I threw myself headlong into the comparative vertebrate anatomy course and soon discovered that I loved anatomy. I also had the kind of mind that could easily memorize the complex anatomy. This older professor was brilliant and charismatic, and through him I fell in love with biology! He took me under his wing and mentored me, helping me see my true potential. I came to realize that I was quite capable of becoming a doctor. Having that professor as my mentor was beyond priceless! I wound up becoming president of the Tri Beta Biological Honor Society, and even sponsored a few guest lectures. I completely turned my GPA around and graduated magna cum laude. Having one or two trusted mentors in your life can truly be a game changer and a life saver. One thing is for sure, there is no shortage of pain and suffering in this world. How great it is to have mentors come alongside young folks to help them find their paths and callings. If you keep shooting for the stars, you might just hit the moon.

CHAPTER 3
DISCOVERING MY DAD

Underneath that mask he wore, who was the real Nick Linkowski? Today, as I revise his story, is the day before what would've been his 101st birthday, had he lived to see it. Dominick (Nick) was born August 27, 1922. As far back as I can remember Dad would always tell us kids that he was going to be 27 on the 27th.

Polish Roots and the Call of Duty

I know precious little about his childhood, or for that matter much about his brothers and sisters and their extended families. That will be one of my projects in the near future. What I do know is Dad grew up in a small apartment in downtown Yonkers right near Getty Square. Essentially an extension of New York City, it was overcrowded with lots of hustle and bustle and stores of all kinds. Dad was the youngest of seven children and I suspect they were living at or just above poverty level. Both of his parents were Polish and while dad spoke Polish fluently, he would never teach us that language. Soon after he graduated from a trade and technical high school, World War II was unfolding. Dad and his three brothers all signed up to serve in the armed forces, as each believed it was his patriotic duty. They were all part of what is believed to be one of the greatest generations ever.

His World of War

Dad became a machinist's mate, first class in the Navy aboard a versatile amphibious vehicle called a landing ship tank (LST). This was the workhorse of landing craft flotilla, filled with smaller crafts, tanks, vehicles, and guns. I combined information from a Navy department resource, coupled with what I learned when I got to interview Dad a few months before his passing, to provide a short summary of LST #355.

His ship and crew participated in D-Day at Red Beach, Safta, in the Bay of Salerno on September 9th, 1943. His LST was ordered to "beach at all costs." Despite stiff German opposition, his crew downed one enemy plane with their anti-aircraft guns. His LST was believed to be the first LST to actually beach at that location, enduring

CHAPTER 3

heavy artillery fire from the opposition. The other dozen LSTs landed on the beach in quick succession. His ship was one of the few LSTs in the entire fleet that got credit for destroying a tank with their 40-millimeter army-type gun.

When I interviewed Dad, he described a graphic scene. When they were almost on the beach, a boat in front of them, as well as a boat behind them, got hit by enemy fire and suffered several casualties. He described the water near the beach as being blood red. To this day it turns my stomach to imagine all the lifeblood of our precious men being spilled into the sea. Soon afterwards, they were off to Palermo, Sicily, despite enemy air attacks and mines.

He also witnessed fighting in Gibraltar. He vividly described a story which happened there when their boat had docked for a short respite. Several crew members were buying eggs from the local townspeople. Somehow Dad had a premonition and yelled to his comrades to run back to the ship. Just imagine soldiers running for their lives in a frenzy! A few split seconds later when they were safely aboard the ship, Nazi aircraft fighters strafed the pier. That story makes me believe in guardian angels! His LST sailed from Falmouth, England, on June 5th, 1944, as a part of force "B" bound for Omaha beach, where he participated in operation Neptune. D-day was the following day. His ship was loaded with field artillery and personnel and was discharging equipment. His ship joined the famous LST shuttle service, which carried the wounded, dead, and enemy prisoners back to England, and heroically completed 44 trips from England to France.

His World of Work

Dad and his brothers returned home and were greeted with a hero's welcome after their time of duty. The celebration, however, was very short-lived. He was hired to work as a machinist for the New York Central Railroad. Eventually he wound up working almost his entire career in the machine shop a few floors below the lower level of Grand Central Terminal in New York City. He would travel by train from Yonkers to the terminal in downtown New York City, catching only a glimpse of the morning light. After that the only light of day he would see would be if he left the terminal to go outside, or when he left for the day in the late afternoon. In that machine shop, Dad found his bliss because there he could perform at his personal best. I still do not understand how he was able to work all day without ever seeing sunlight. I believe he was a true artist at his craft, which went way above and beyond the mechanical work. He just loves to what he did.

CHAPTER 3

He was admired and respected by all who knew him. He was a man who could fix just about anything. Mom would always say, "If dad can't fix it, then throw it away." I got to witness this up close and personal. One of my uncles had given me his tired old 1963 Simca when I turned sixteen. The Simca was a very small box-like French 4-cylinder car. That dull, red-colored car was on its last leg, but it was my first car, and I absolutely loved it. It was a four-on-the-floor stick shift manual transmission, and what fun it was learning to drive it! That was until one day one of the pistons blew up, and the car was disabled. We started hunting for a replacement engine and lo and behold, we found the same make and model car just a couple of miles away. We went to visit this elderly Frenchman who owned it, and he sold it to us for a nominal fee. I watched in awe and helped Dad dissemble the entire engine, replacing the broken piston and piston rings. Dad performed this feat without any type of manual whatsoever. He just had that confidence, knowledge, and experience to get the job done. I enjoyed driving that vehicle for a few more years, with the highlight being taking two of my buddies on a camping trip to Cape Cod. Nothing like sleeping in our sleeping bags on Race Point Beach overnight, only to be awakened by the state trooper, telling us to pack up and move.

Shell Shock and Alcohol Changed Him

Dad would use all his vacation time to take care of us kids. Most of the time, Dad was a simple gentle soul, generous and full of integrity and kindness. Then came the dramatic shift when the generational curse of alcohol addiction entered the picture.

Dad's attempted suicide showcased just how bad PTSD can be. During World War II, the term "shell shock" was replaced by the term combat stress reaction (CSR), also known as battle or combat fatigue. PTSD became a formal diagnosis in the *Diagnostic and Statistical Manual of Mental Disorders, Third Edition (DSMIII)*, published in 1980. To my knowledge and belief, Dad was one of the innumerable soldiers from World War II who had severe PTSD and was never treated. It has become very clear to me that life for Dad was so painful that numbing his feelings with alcohol likely provided at least temporary relief from the pain. I will never know just how wide and deep that pain was. Maybe when we rejoin in heaven, I will ask him, but by then it will have been forgotten.

Finally, around 1986 my family had an intervention with Dad, and miraculously, he agreed to go into rehab for approximately one month. He became sober and an active member of Alcoholic Anonymous, which he attended regularly. Dad remained alcohol free for the next 20 years until his passing in November 2006. In his final years, Dad had some chronic breathing problems, which were probably secondary to his habit of smoking both cigars and pipes through the years. In addition to that, I believe he likely inhaled toxic fumes and particles at his jobs in the war, and while working underground as a machinist. This pre-dated the multiple safety regulations that have thankfully been put in place since then.

Degeneration and Dementia

Dad was diagnosed with Parkinson's disease and as the years went by, he waxed in and out of progressive dementia. There is one story about Dad I never get tired of. A few years before he died, I had spent about five days at my parents' home in Yonkers while attending a radiology conference in New Jersey. One morning, after I had left for the day, he turned to mom and asked, "Who is that nice young man staying with us?" Mom promptly responded, "That's our son, Greg." I personally love that story in that Dad was unbiased and actually thought I was a nice guy. Thanks Dad, I'll take that compliment any day.

Dad's medical problems worsened in November 2006, and after falling at home, had to be hospitalized.

DISCOVERING MY DAD

My brother called me at my job in California on a Friday afternoon and said Dad had just been admitted to the hospital and he thought I had better come back, it was serious. I flew back to New York that night on the Redeye. Saturday and Sunday I spent visiting my family along with short visits with Dad. The following Monday is a day I will never forget. His medical situation had been stabilized and the following day he was going to have an evaluation by hospice for home hospice care. Up to that time, Mom had taken excellent care of Dad in his last couple of years, even performing a lot of nursing duties. This, of course, came with Mom's sassy attitude just to keep things lively. Monday night Mom, as well as all my siblings, were exhausted from continual visits with Dad. I told Mom I felt I should go to the hospital and visit him.

There he was, semi-comatose, tousled grey and black hair, lying in the hospital bed. I fondly recall feeding him some cranberry juice, which he gladly sipped through a straw. It felt to me like I was taking care of a small child. Then suddenly, I found myself saying these following words. "You know, Dad, it's OK to just let go. We all love you." Then as if on automatic pilot, I recited the Lord's prayer and the Saint Francis of Assisi prayer loudly enough for even his roommate to hear. Just before I left, I kissed Dad gently on the forehead and thought to myself, *wow that was a nice visit.* I went to bed that night looking forward to being there for the hospice evaluation the following morning. I was at a quick work out around 9 AM when my brother called me and informed me that Dad had died a couple of hours before. Then came a true "aha" moment in my life. It became crystal clear that God had inspired my visit the night before to give Dad a great send off and blessing. There is no explanation but that my words were inspired by God. Trust that what I am telling you is the God's honest truth.

The Reflection of the Man I Love

As I reflect on the man my Dad was, I love and admire him even more and more as time goes by. Dad had several great one-liner phrases over the last few years of his life, and the one I like best is, "I'm still here." The last few times I heard that phrase, I felt like Dad couldn't believe he was still here on earth, ha ha! Yes, Dad, you are still here and will remain in our hearts forever. In some ways, despite his terrible PTSD and addiction, Dad helped me become the man that I am today. His kindness and generosity are traits that I am proud to continue. While I emulate those valuable traits, he also taught me what not to do as a father. I believe that each generation is charged with doing better than the generation before. Dad, I am grateful for having had you as my father, and look forward to reuniting with you in heaven, when my time comes. Having Jesus as my Lord and Savior assures me of that.

CHAPTER 4
BONDING THROUGH FISHING (IF THERE'S WATER...)

My dad's favorite hobby was passed on to me and became my favorite hobby as well. That hobby is sport or recreational fishing. Early on in my childhood, Dad began taking all four of us children on fishing trips. As the years passed, it ended up being just us three boys, then years later often just me and my dad. Dad would sometimes say that if there was water in it, he would fish there. To this day, I still feel a connection with my dad whenever I go fishing. What a wonderful feeling!

As a young boy, I fondly remember walking with Dad down the hill from our house to the Sawmill River Creek. Using dough balls as bait, we would sometimes catch carp that weighed as much as nine or ten pounds. As we walked back up the hill, we would stop at our neighbor's house and give them the carp, which they thoroughly enjoyed. We had so many great times fishing at a local reservoir, Grassy Sprain Reservoir. There we would usually catch bass as well as white perch. One night I was pulling in a small sunfish when suddenly, I had something much larger on the line. That sunfish had been swallowed whole by a large snapping turtle. We landed it, then watched as it made its journey back into the water, hissing and snapping along the way. Progress came, the highway was built along that reservoir, and they closed it permanently to fishing. That was a sad time in my life, and I truly miss those special times. I have driven along that highway multiple times and feel nostalgic, still grateful to have those cherished memories.

A Glimpse of Heaven

I love being near or on the water in a boat, where my mind gets lulled into a blissful state. I concentrate on my fishing rod and whatever bait or lure I am using but relax at the same time. Just when you least expect it, wham! A fish hits and you're off to the races. There is no feeling in the world like the sheer joy of playing a fish and landing it. It's a time when everyone's defenses are down, and we are all out there just to have fun. Those times were so sacred and special as we got to know each other, and even ourselves better. For me, it was never just about catching fish, but it was about the experience,

CHAPTER 4

like catching a glimpse of heaven. Feeling a sense of calm and well-being, fishing was when time stood still, and I could feel at one with nature and God and rediscover my sense of purpose. For me fishing was a very real form of meditation and a way to communicate with God. I discovered the best version of my dad during these times when he allowed me to truly get to know him in this safe and comfortable environment.

Glory Days

As I grew older, our trips became more focused. Early spring found us fishing for trout in rivers, streams, and reservoirs, and it didn't matter much to us whether it was cold or rainy. Summertime was spent at several lakes catching bass and whatever else would bite.

I love to reminisce about our many summer trips to Long Island Sound. We would often rent a rowboat out of New Rochelle, New York. Dad brought along his small outboard motor, attaching it to the back of the boat, and away we would go. We were indeed proud fisherman, and although we had one of the smallest boats on the sound, to me it felt like being on a yacht. One summer day we had a once-in-a-lifetime trip experience when we encountered a large school of bluefish. Baitfish were frantically jumping out of the water and seagulls swarmed and dove to the water to catch and eat those fish. I felt a constant adrenaline rush as we used our jigs, and we almost always had one or two fish on our lines simultaneously. Believe it or not, we caught a total of 38 bluefish that day! A record! I'm not really sure why we kept all of those fish, but somehow, we found a home for all of them.

Some of my greatest fishing trips were in the fall when we would go out to Playland at Rye, New York, where an old Italian man had a fleet of row boats for rent. We would buy a bucket of fiddler crabs and catch black fish off the rocky shores, all the while gazing at the amusement park in the background. I couldn't help but think this was as good as it gets. There were times that Dad mentored me, sharing his extensive knowledge and experience of the type fishing that we were doing. I believe my dad had trouble sharing his emotions, but that was not the case when we were fishing. His guard was down, and he became larger than life. He had limitless patience when my line was snagged, had a tangle, or I needed more bait. I felt like he shared the very essence of who he really was underneath the exterior. My fishing experiences have affected me so deeply that I've taken my wife Lynn and my children fishing many times. It has

CHAPTER 4

become very important for me to pass on this familial tradition, legacy, and nuggets of joy.

Lessons in the Rowboat

One of the only times I got acquainted with two of my dad's older brothers was around the age of 15 when Dad, his brothers and I went up to Quincy, Massachusetts, to catch flounder. I shared the same rowboat with his older brother. There's nothing like getting to know someone when you are both in a small boat together. Even to this day I calm my mind before going to sleep or taking a nap by visualizing being in one of those row boats. I have a lot of respect for those who make a living as commercial fishermen, and I am proud to be a recreational fisherman. Remember, some of Jesus' disciples were fishermen. I am fond of the saying that the Lord does not deduct from the hours of man those spent in fishing. That's a very good reason to spend more time fishing as I enter my fourth quarter.

Fishing to me is analogous to searching for the meaning of life. I believe it is so important for the elders and our generation to pass on hobbies and the like to the next generation that they are passionate about to help leave a positive legacy. For me, it has become very important to leave a legacy of truly serving others without expectation

BONDING THROUGH FISHING (IF THERE'S WATER...)

in return. I believe that one way to bring true happiness into our lives is to be more like Jesus, whom I believe to be the greatest servant who ever lived. All of us either have had or will have difficult circumstances in life. The important thing is how we respond to those circumstances. Will you become bitter or better? Maintaining a positive attitude is key to developing a life with meaning.

CHAPTER 5
THE LEGEND OF MOTHER TERESA (NO, NOT THAT ONE)

Trying to define my mother Teresa is like trying to catch lightning in a bottle. She was a very tough, strong, faithful, and loving lady with a big heart. She was also a compulsive coupon collector, and if you rubbed her the wrong way, she could be really cranky. She was born in 1927 in Yonkers, New York, the oldest of nine children. Along with her parents and aunt, she lived in a three-bedroom 1100 square-foot row house in downtown Yonkers. Sleeping arrangements must have been much more than cozy. And in the early years the only bathroom they had was an outhouse. Just imagine going outside during a blizzard and freezing all the way there and back, not to mention being bare-bottomed in an unheated one-holer! Brr! Later in her childhood they built a small bathroom in a far corner of the basement. In her words, "Growing up was something else." She became the elder protector of her brothers and sisters, as well as defending herself. She relayed a story when one winter day, while walking to school, a neighborhood boy taunted her by taking her hat, and tossing it off a bridge. That young boy got the surprise of his life when the next time she saw him, "I knocked his tooth out when I whacked him!" Surely her childhood must have been sacrificed as she became a little mommy to her younger siblings. That's just how Mom rolled.

She Knew How to Work

Soon came the Great Depression. Most families were poverty stricken and they queued for free food. Unemployment was rampant and people were hungry. There were mostly men on the bread lines, but Mom also waited on those lines. You had better believe she was as tough as any of the men and could hold her own anywhere. She also had an amazing work ethic. During summer vacations when she was just 13 years old, she worked in the diet kitchen at St. John's Hospital. The usual schedule was to report each morning at 5:30 AM. First order of the day was to crush and squeeze a giant crate of oranges to make fresh-squeezed orange juice for the patients. After washing all the dishes by hand and cleaning up, Mom had a few hours off. Her job description required her to report back in the mid-afternoon for the dinner part of the shift. Back in

CHAPTER 5

those good old days, there was no such thing as a day off, not even one. Finally, one day she got up the courage to ask for a day off. This was her supervisor's response, "Don't you know that sick people need to eat on Sunday, too?"

Terry was off to business high school at age 14. That same year she landed a job at a bank in Getty Square and was quickly promoted to bank teller. She was allowed to leave school in the early afternoon to work at the bank and also worked there all day on Saturday. As you might suspect, she gave all her money to her mom to help run the house. In return she received a meager allowance. After skipping a grade in high school, she graduated at age 16.

Take a Letter, Teresa

One day her uncle John saw her looking at want ads in the paper. He was an old railroad man and said to her, "Why don't you try the railroad?" So she asked him where to go. Equipped with instructions and a couple of dollars, she and her 14-year-old sister Agnes got all dolled up, white gloves and all, like two babes from the woods and traveled by train down to Grand Central terminal, where she presented herself to the chief of police for the railroad. He really put her to the test by rattling off a quick letter, half expecting her to just sit there and wobble. However, she had taken the letter by stenography and typed out a perfect letter, done business style. She was hired for the job as secretary on the spot. Legend has it that she once won a contest in New York City using her stenography skills. Later in life, she would listen to new songs on the radio and learn them by taking stenography. One day a company big shot invited her to work with the railroad management team. She followed and eventually became executive assistant to several CEOs.

The Way to a Man's Heart

Over time she made a number of friends and one bright sunny day, a mutual friend introduced Mom and Dad. Their romance developed slowly over time and eventually there was the big date, when she invited him over to her house and cooked for him. Mom and Dad married in February 1950. Her first pregnancy ended up with the miscarriage of twin boys at around five months; unfortunately, commonplace back in the early 50s. Then came my older sister, and a couple of years later in January 1954 I arrived during a blizzard, which may explain a lot about me! My two brothers followed. Once we were all in school, Mom really had a juggling act after returning to work part time. A real dilemma was presented when she was asked

CHAPTER 5

to work full-time. Thank God for amazing friends. Her best friend, Tonya insisted that all us kids go over to her house after school for a couple of hours during the week, as they lived very close to our school. My youngest brother was in kindergarten with her son, and the rest of us were in grade school. She was a godsend, and her children were our age, so we had instant playmates. That situation lasted for a few good years. Other ladies and a couple of older girls from our neighborhood also pitched in to help while we were still too young to be left on our own.

Provision Was Always There

Our family was lower middle class. On occasion early on I would wish for a bit more food like chicken at supper, but we never went hungry. Later in life, Mom's words reminded us that "whenever we wanted anything substantial, we got it when we needed it." She was super thrifty and could stretch a buck further than anybody I have ever met. It was as if she grew money on a hidden tree somewhere. Another of mom's sayings was, "I never wanted to see anybody in debt." To this day I do not understand how she and Dad were able to pay for my college and medical school leaving me debt free. Mom and Dad also helped all three of my siblings financially and left us each a modicum of inheritance. Lynn and I are following that tradition with joy.

Money aside, she left us much richer with her great wit and sense of humor. As Mom grew older, she became more fully human in many ways. Some people become cranky and bitter as they age, but not Mom. She was a lector at the Catholic church for many years, up to age 93. She was also in several prayer groups. As the Wizard of Oz would say, she was "a good deed doer." Even after she retired, she spent several years keeping the books, and helping one of my brothers with his business venture. If Mom could help a family in crisis, she was all in.

The End of a Legacy

Mom remained in good health until just after her 93rd birthday. Then as if out of nowhere, end-stage congestive heart failure reared its ugly head. Over the span of about six months, she went through a revolving door of hospitalizations, rehab, and short stays at home. Her giving heart was becoming worn out and tired and it became painfully clear that there was no way she could any longer live independently in the two-story house of my childhood. That home had a single small bathroom up several stairs and there was no bedroom downstairs. I envisioned

CHAPTER 5

this as an accident waiting to happen. She would even tell us, "I'm going to die in this house." My response was, "Not on my watch." All of us siblings pitched in to help, and eventually Mom moved into a top-notch assisted living facility. That undoubtedly enhanced the quality and length of her meaningful life.

The sentinel event occurred when she fell one night which led to other medical problems in rapid sequence; soon she was in a coma at the hospital. I was blessed and honored to have been her healthcare proxy. I was quite familiar with her medical situation and her expressed wishes. A few days after being on dilaudid, valium, and IV sustenance, I got a call from the palliative care nurse practitioner. It was crystal clear to me that Mom would not have wanted to prolong or extend her remaining life in a coma, as her soul was ready to go on to glory. My siblings and I stood united as we agreed to the palliative care team plan. I had previously served on the ethics committee at my hospital, and I have learned to honor the wishes of the patient. It is ideal to have the wishes of both the patient and the family in synchrony and unison.

We each had time to say our final goodbyes and Lynn even sang some spiritual hymns. Each of us prayed in our own way beside her in her hospital room. I spent two nights by her bedside in the hospital a few nights before she died. It was very special to me just to hold her hand and lay my left hand on her right arm as I slept for part of the night. The priest who eulogized her said she had an indomitable spirit. She was very strong but could also be very stubborn. She remained a pillar in the church for decades, demonstrating her faith not just by words but by actions. She would reach out to new visitors and introduce herself. Parishioners would sometimes tell the priest that they decided to make this their home church because of Mom's kindness towards them. Mom's loving spirit and generosity endured till the end of her life.

As it turns out, Mom was the last of Lynn's and my parents to pass on to eternity. Lynn and I are now the elders in our families. My Mom's death has reminded me of my own mortality. Now I face certain questions about myself. How will I be remembered? What kind of legacy will I leave? As I reflect on Mom's life, I love and cherish her even more now that she has gone on to her eternal reward. Thank you, Mom, for a life well lived. You have certainly given me a generous heart and inspired me to persevere through any difficulty. In the end, it really is about faith, hope, and love. The greatest of these is love. Mom, you truly modeled a life worth living with how you love others. Now it is our mission to carry that forward.

CHAPTER 6
WE'VE BEEN WORKING ON THE RAILROAD

"All aboard!" roared the conductor of the Hudson line train. I grew up in a railroad working family. My parents and siblings all worked for the railroad in various capacities and had successful careers. My dad was a very gifted machinist. My mom was a talented secretary who eventually worked her way up the ladder to become executive assistant to a few different transportation superintendents. Each of my parents had the potential to have gone much further in their professional endeavors had they lived in a later era and gone to college; however, each of them played well the hand that was dealt to them. College never became an option for either of them. That's just the way things were back then; people just worked hard for a living, and essentially lived from paycheck to paycheck.

WE'VE BEEN WORKING ON THE RAILROAD

The Railroad Network

Our family built quite a railroad history through the years. The railroad had quite a history itself. The familiar Metro North is a descendant of commuter rail services dating back to 1832. Penn Central acquired New York Central when it became bankrupt and formed Conrail. Then in 1983 the MTA took on Conrail and merged into the current entity known as Metro North.

Everyone knows in many areas of life it's not so much what you know, but who you know. Connections really do matter. My mother used her influence on my behalf. All my summer jobs between the ages of 18 and 23 were spent working for the railroad. I spent one summer working at the 125th Street train station in East Harlem Manhattan. I was astonished when I discovered that I was assigned the role of clerk/assistant to the supervisor of the bridge and building department. There were all kinds of skilled laborers in the department, especially carpenters. I would keep their timecards and do whatever chores were assigned to me by my supervisor. He was a tough old man who kept everybody in line but deep down inside he had a big heart. Sometimes I mediated between the workers and the supervisor. There was a high crime rate in the area and railroad police patrolled around the station on a regular basis.

CHAPTER 6

Oddly enough, there were two college girls from Nebraska working in a small shop in the middle of this train station. It was strange to imagine two young blonde-haired, blue-eyed girls from the Midwest working in downtown New York as their summer jobs, yet they seemed to really enjoy themselves. Because of the tough area I didn't venture out far or often from that train station, but I did find time to go to their store, and even flirt a bit with both of them. I developed more street smarts that summer in the inner city, but little did I know that just a few short years later I would be doing my OB/GYN rotation as a medical student at Lincoln Hospital in the South Bronx, just a couple of miles away.

Two of my summer jobs were working as a custodian. The first time I was a night porter, working the night shift with two older fellows who were nearing retirement. It was a very cushy job, with lots of time spent reading, and, oh yes, occasionally sweeping up different train stations and emptying garbage. We would usually work for about 30 minutes and take a break for about 30 minutes. I was to find out later that those jobs are few and far between. The second summer of working as a janitor was just the opposite. I actually had to work for a living, imagine that! You haven't lived until you've cleaned up dank foul smelling urine stains off the walls and floors in the hallway at Yonkers train station! That was a very humbling experience for me, and I am grateful for that experience. That particular summer we would travel as far north as Poughkeepsie train station. I didn't think being a janitor was my true passion, but I still did my very best. There is a lot of truth in "Whatever you do, work at it with all your heart, as working for the Lord, not for human masters (Colossians 3: 23).

The Railroad "Gang"

The two summers that I spent working on the track gang were far more colorful than the summers working as a custodian. There was still plenty of racial tension in New York back in the early 70s. Almost all the workers were men of color. There were Sicilians and Puerto Ricans who would gravitate on one bus, and African American men who would be on the other bus. We few Caucasian boys would go on either bus. The nicknames that some of them had were unforgettable. One fellow was nicknamed Frog, another one was Meatloaf, and yet another was called Cornbread. One of the Puerto Rican assistant supervisors used to address us simply as "Buddy-buddy," but in a rapid staccato fashion. You can't make this stuff up. These fellows were strong as oxen and sprinkled in the group

CHAPTER 6

were a few sluggish white college boys. The foreman of the gang nick-named us Young Bloods. He was small, but a very tough guy with an attitude half the size of New Jersey. He was fearless and would confront anybody who misbehaved. One day while working in the South Bronx a couple of kids hurled glass bottles at us from an overpass. The oldest member of the track gang was a fellow who was called Pop. He was probably 65 years old, give or take a few years. One summer day Pop meandered away from the gang and was about 50 yards away. His back faced an oncoming commuter train flying down the rails at 50 miles an hour. He was on that same track! We leapt into action and yelled to him, but he couldn't hear us. Merely a few seconds away from his imminent death I swung my arms and hands wildly over my head gesturing him to move. He peeked over his shoulder just as the train was about to kill him and jumped off the track with superhuman strength. While difficult to prove with certainty, I think an angel might have lifted him up as I never saw Pop move so quickly!

I also recall working with an Italian city boy from the South Bronx. One day he told me about his recent trip to Mexico, where he visited an ancient Mayan city. He referred to that city as Chicken Pizza (really Chichen Itzá). I still laugh when I reminisce about that time. My mother was able to get my dear friend and medical school classmate a job with me on the track gang for the final summer. I observed his true grit as he worked every bit as hard as I did. I'm grateful that to this day we remain friends for life.

I truly cherish the memories of my varied and colorful summer jobs and experiences working for the railroad. They helped mold me into the man I am today. I have a much deeper appreciation for the folks who do manual labor and other hard service-oriented jobs. My parents instilled a very strong work ethic in me that certainly helped me persevere and never give up during medical school, in my residency and fellowship, in my marriage and beyond. I will be eternally grateful for that. Winston Churchill is quoted as saying "never give in, never give in, never, never, never, never—in nothing, great or small, large or petty—never give in except to convictions of honor and good sense."

CHAPTER 7
CALIFORNIA DREAMIN'

Without a doubt, one of the greatest adventures I have ever experienced was in the summer of 1974 at the ripe young age of 20. I devoted the first half of that summer to working on the railroad and at the deli to make some dough. My two best friends and I decided that we would like nothing better than to take a long road trip across the country to visit this majestic land of ours, especially California. We traveled in style as the parents of one of my buddies allowed us to use their sleek and roomy Chrysler Newport sedan. When our departure date arrived, we packed the sedan, loaded to the gills, and embarked on our once-in-a-lifetime road trip. We could hardly wait to see this beautiful American countryside. Our dreams would soon transform into reality before our very eyes.

CALIFORNIA DREAMIN'

Cornfields and All-nighters

We chose to take the northern route to the West Coast. As we drove through Pennsylvania, I was awestruck with the greenery and beauty of the rolling hills. A couple of days later we gazed at mile after mile of cornfields in Iowa and Nebraska. We took turns driving till the wee hours of the morning, stopping to sleep in the car for only a couple of hours, then after we arose and had breakfast, just like Willie Nelson, were on the road again.

Sleeping Bags and Fresh Fish

We planned this vacation with our ultra-low budget in mind. Even though we couldn't spend money hand over fist, we all felt like kings. Back in those days, it was no problem for us to sleep in sleeping bags in a tent, or sometimes simply sleep in the car. We had youth on our side, and we were strong and resilient. We traveled onward to Colorado where we found an available campsite in Estes Park. I still remember the picturesque beauty of the beautiful valley surrounded by snow-covered mountains. Longfellow once said, "Into each life some rain must fall," and indeed that turned out to be the case one cold and rainy night. Thank God the tent kept us warm and dry. While there we went hiking and horseback riding in the Colorado hills.

Our next stop was Yellowstone National Park, where we set up camp in Grant Village. I felt like I died and gone to heaven as we sat in a rowboat on a crystal-clear lake in Yellowstone catching cutthroat trout with the afternoon sun beaming down on us. Fresh trout cooked over the fireplace for dinner was quite the delight.

Old Faithful and the PNW

We visited the thermal springs which displayed rich colors of red, yellow, blue, and orange. That was only eclipsed by witnessing Old Faithful erupt, right on time of course. In the park we met some fellow travelers and broke bread together. Being at Yellowstone was both exhilarating and relaxing for me and is one place that I would visit again in a heartbeat; however, the next time I would sincerely prefer to stay in a hotel.

We ventured north to our next stop, Glacier National Park in northwest Montana. We camped out near Saint Mary's Lake, a true glacial lake with blue-green pristine water. We journeyed onward to Spokane, Washington, to visit the 1974 Expo World's Fair. The theme that year was ecology, and the venue displayed a variety of ecological exhibits. They were interesting and educational, but my most memorable experience happened at one of the game booths. I felt drawn to play this particular game which required tossing a quarter onto a shallow glass cookie tray. The trick was to make the quarter land and stay put on the glass tray without sliding off. By the way, this is much harder than it appears at first sight. I performed this feat successfully on my first toss, and while I would like to claim it as the luck of the Irish, I happen to be all Polish. I was awarded this oversized stuffed dog as my prize. The only trouble was that if we were to take it with us, it would take up almost half the back seat. There was just no way we could fit that in the car which was already chock full of our belongings and three guys. Just then, this cute young lady happened by and stopped to admire my new prize. On the spur of the moment, I decided to hand it off to her. My dog had found a permanent home! She beamed with delight and left hugging her new stuffed doggy. I tried that game about six more times, total fail. The lesson I learned was don't argue with success. When it comes to gambling, it's best to walk away while you are ahead of the game. Otherwise, you can refer to the song "the gambler" recorded most famously by Kenny Rogers.

CHAPTER 7

The Golden Coast

Sleeping in the driver's seat of the car was a unique experience. Although I woke up facing the steering wheel, I actually slept very well. Today's theme was, "Drive till we drop." The one memorable thing that I recall about being in Portland was buying a new tire for my buddy's car at the Sears store. We felt like we struck gold once we entered California. Our first arrival was at Redwood Rest Resort in Klamath. We hiked to the Klamath River, but it was way too expensive for us to purchase temporary fishing licenses. Little did I know that 25 years later I would catch steelhead on a boat in that same river with a fishing guide. We stared in awe at the majestic redwoods at Ladybird Johnson Memorial Grove, where a few of the trees are estimated to be 2000 years old. The next day we decided to experience what it was like to be in the polar bear club, and we swam in the frigid Northern California coastal waters. We simply had to spend an entire day and night in San Francisco, the majestic city by the Bay. After booking a room at Holiday Inn in Chinatown we feasted on delicious Chinese food. The next day we parked at Fort Mason and strolled along the boardwalk with a bird's eye view of the Golden Gate Bridge, Alcatraz, and Sausalito from across the Bay. Fisherman's Wharf and

Ghirardelli Square were enjoyable as well as our visit to Haight Ashbury. I had assumed that this would be the only time that I would visit San Francisco, however, a decade later I was proven wrong as Lynn and I wound up living in that city for three years as newlyweds.

If you ever have the time and want to experience a truly amazing scenic highway, take US Hwy 1 from Santa Cruz south to San Luis Obispo. The steep rugged coastal scenery is unbelievable. The "high point" was Big Sur. This is where the Santa Lucia Mountains rise abruptly from the Pacific Ocean. The town itself is approximately 144 feet above sea level with the area around it ranging from 76 feet to 2137 feet. It is glorious and majestic.

Little Italy in LA

One of my buddies was 100% Italian. Our next destination was Gardena in the LA area where his aunt and uncle, the "macaroni relatives," had a fabulous meal prepared and waiting for us. We enjoyed visiting that evening and soon all three of us were getting tired and ready to go to a nice warm bed, however, we soon discovered that there was a definite misunderstanding. The uncle assumed that since we traveled across country that we must have traveled in a van and that was where we would sleep. Of course, that

CHAPTER 7

is what most people did on a cross country trip, but we were the exceptions. We, on the other hand, had assumed that they had plenty of room for us in their home. Both assumptions turned out to be very wrong. They offered us what they had which was simply a small guest room with a single bed. We wound up with two cots and one bed and rotated during the three nights we were there, so each of us had our night in a real bed. I thoroughly enjoyed the day we spent in Disneyland, as well as the next day visiting Manhattan Beach, Hollywood, and Universal Studios. Our friend had been sick on and off for a few days before arriving in California, perhaps with some car sickness and probably some home sickness as well. He decided to remain with his relatives for a few more days, and then fly back home to New York.

Gambling Doesn't Pay, It Costs

I don't remember being sad when we left him. All things considered, he did what was right for him to do and I respected that. The two of us were back on the road again, headed for Las Vegas. Going there was probably the first and only real mistake we made on our trip. There we were, two young New York dudes, barely wet behind the ears, going into the casinos. I was carrying a grand total of

$26 in my pocket. Shortly afterwards, I lost nearly all of it playing blackjack. Relegated to the nickel slot machine, I won 90 nickels, then methodically used all of them up until I was penniless. We did see a live show with Bill Cosby and the Letterman, and that was a really big deal. We left Las Vegas with our pockets lighter, but we were richer for the experience.

The Colorful Southwest

Our next stop was the Grand Canyon in Arizona. It's hard to imagine that the Colorado River spent an estimated 3 million years gnawing away at the rock to form the Canyon; with some parts being about 4000 feet below the top of the Canyon. The predominant colors were deep red, reddish brown, yellow, green, and purple. We then drove onward through Arizona and New Mexico, headed for New Orleans. One day we traveled about 700 miles. The car was barely drivable as we limped into this very small town called Claude, Texas, nestled in the Panhandle of northwest Texas. Back in 1974, the population was 1000 people or less. We were quite concerned that the transmission might be faulty, but it turned out that one of the exhaust pipes was blocked. It did take a full day to get the replacement pipe delivered and installed, so we enjoyed visiting

CHAPTER 7

with some of the locals who were a very nice bunch of people. They say things are bigger and better in Texas and we agreed. It was a very picturesque state.

The Lush South

Louisiana was lush and verdant with countless bayous. I remember smelling the rich moisture in the air. We finally arrived in New Orleans, a fabulous city. My favorite streets in the French Quarter were Royal Street and Bourbon Street. We stayed in a picturesque hotel on Royal Street for only $30 and we had two rooms and a balcony. The French Quarter was alive with jazz, rock, and people singing, dancing, and enjoying themselves. The view of New Orleans from the 33rd floor of the tower was priceless!

Soon we headed for Great Smokey Mountain National Park on the Tennessee/North Carolina border. We found a lovely campsite at Smokemont. That area abounded with black bear, and we even saw one rummaging through garbage cans looking for dinner. That park was a mere 740 miles from our home in Yonkers and we traveled back home the following day.

The more I reflect on my life at age 70, I am more and more grateful for that trip and all its memories. All in all, there were 10,000 miles worth of memories. Today while there is time, be inventive and create your own memories to cherish moving forward. Make time for family, eating together, creating family traditions. Live life while you can! Create those high point moments and celebrate special moments, staying connected to family and friends. Nobody except God knows your exact number of days. You don't want to be one of those people whose deathbed lament is that they didn't spend more time with their family.

CHAPTER 8
THE VALLEY OF THE SHADOW OF...HELL?

Going through my internship in internal medicine was like walking through the valley of hell. Imagine being fresh out of medical school in 1980. I had learned a vocabulary of several thousand medical terms that nobody outside of medicine knew or wanted to know. I also had certain skills, and I knew how to perform a history and a physical exam. Without a doubt, I was still wet behind the ears. One spring day our entire fourth year medical student class assembled, and we each received notification of the medical institution where we had been matched for our internships. I had a sinking feeling about where I had been matched as I was assigned to work in a large tertiary care hospital in Philadelphia. At the end of June, I loaded up my Honda Prelude and made the trip to Philadelphia. I was assigned a small apartment in the residence hall across the street from the hospital. The first day of internship arrived in short order and I looked the part wearing my

THE VALLEY OF THE SHADOW OF...HELL?

long white coat with my name embroidered in script over my front left pocket; my stethoscope in my right-side pocket. My resident handed me a list of about 15 patients on the oncology ward. I was responsible for following each one, and it seemed that each patient was sicker than the one before. I fell into a deep temporary depression and was filled with fear and anxiety. What would happen if somebody died on my watch? I felt inadequate and ill-prepared to handle this monumental task; however, the fighter inside me took command. I forced myself to stay on the ward until late at night, learning all I could about each patient. I followed my resident around like a puppy, following all his commands. He was the captain of the ship, and I was his first mate. I began to get the feel of the job, and later that month felt like I could do this job. I was slowly becoming more and more confident as I repeated several tasks and gained some valuable experience. Then one day during attending rounds, I was humiliated in front of the group when I was asked a medical question about the patient, and I did not know the answer. In medical jargon they call this being pimped. I felt angry afterwards and vowed never to let this happen again. I channeled my anger into productivity and I over-prepared, just waiting for the next opportunity. When that time came and he singled me out, everyone was astonished with my level of knowledge, and I had my victory. As the years of my post-graduate training rolled by I discovered that pimping was rather common and often used as a training technique, almost like a negative reinforcement.

Finding My feet...on Roller Skates

Several months later I began a two-month rotation in a satellite community hospital. My new resident was a wonderful man who was both kind and gracious to me. We were in a medical situation that was analogous to being in a M.A.S.H. unit in wartime. Both of us were stretched beyond our capabilities. His primary assignment was to remain in the emergency room helping the doctors there, along with triaging patients to determine who needed hospitalization. I oversaw all of the patients on three different floors: between 100 to150 patients by my estimate. I was also responsible to "work up" the new patients admitted to the hospital. In the chain of command, I was assigned two senior 4th-year medical students. My bright idea was for them to function as sub-interns. In short order, I devised my survival plan. I congratulated each one of them as I promoted them to act as if they were my interns. They worked up the new patients who were just admitted, and I supervised them as if I were the resident,

THE VALLEY OF THE SHADOW OF...HELL?

writing only a brief note. During this survival experience we became a quite cohesive team, like iron sharpening iron. It was as if we were on roller skates; I raced between patients, starting IV's, adjusting medications, and supervising the medical students. Many times, we had things almost in control and orderly and all of a sudden, wham! The code beeper screamed out and we all had to drop everything and run to help the team resuscitate a dying patient. These days I refrain from watching medical drama shows, I really lived it!

The month that I spent working in the respiratory ICU remains in my memory as a blur. For the entire month I was in the unit 24 hours straight, then off the following 24 hours. Whatever sleep I did get in the ICU was full of nightmares. I immediately learned that the way to survive that experience was to follow and to do whatever the nurses told me to do. Each of those nurses had knowledge and experience way beyond my own and my admiration and respect for nurses remains quite high to this day. Truly they are some of the biggest heroes in the medical community, always front and center in the drama of life and death in the hospital. A good nurse is worth her weight in gold and then some.

My internship would not have been complete without going through it with a fellow intern named Charlie. We

CHAPTER 8

were from different backgrounds but boy, did we hit it off as two wild and crazy guys! Each of us was paid a total of $10,000 for the internship year, and needless to say money was tight. One day I invited Charlie over for dinner. Going through the grocery store the cheapest protein I could find were chicken backs. I bought a package of them and broiled them up. We both feasted on them, but he has never let me live that down. We both potentiated each other to really live and laugh through our misery and victories. The culture, times, immaturity, stress, and a whole host of factors made this a season of life that can be only lived through once, thank God. Even though I rarely acknowledged God during this time, I am certain that He was watching over me to see me through one of the toughest years of my entire life. God was certainly walking beside me as I transitioned from surviving into thriving, and although I matured somewhat during that year, there was much more to follow. "I have told you these things, so that in me, you may have peace. In this world you will have trouble. But take heart! I have overcome the world" (John 16: 33).

CHAPTER 9
RADIOLOGY, RESIDENCY, AND FELLOWSHIP

June 1981 finally arrived, and the last month of my internship was a cakewalk since I wound up doing an elective in radiology. No more on-call for a couple of months! Making it through that year of internship left me feeling victorious and joyful. Of course, this came after I understood the rhythm and got the hang of it. I was grateful to have finished this commitment and to top it off I was about to embark on a new adventure!

California Here We Come

Surprisingly, my dad volunteered to drive cross-country with me, certainly a once-in-a- lifetime trip with the both of us together. My red 1980 Honda Prelude was stuffed to the gills with all my necessary belongings, filling the tiny trunk and backseat. That Honda was only a two-seat vehicle. It had a backseat although realistically you could

CHAPTER 9

only place infants or small children in that location. We headed off for California and Dad wanted to see only two sites in the country, the Grand Canyon and Las Vegas. At face value, that seemed like quite a dichotomy. However, that's what he requested and that's what we did. Dad wound up being a great traveling companion and while he didn't say very much, the peaceful look on his face said everything. Even now over 40 years later and Dad having passed, I still fondly remember how enjoyable it was to have him along as my travel partner.

Imaging, Intuition, and Inspiration

I easily found an apartment for rent in Huntington Beach just one mile from the beach on the Pacific Ocean. I cannot tell you the number of times I jogged down to the beach, running all the way to the Huntington Beach pier and back again. While I was sad to see Dad off at the airport, I was excited to dive into my residency in diagnostic radiology. I can tell you from personal experience that a good cross-sectional radiologist has the ability to diagnose based on x-rays, ultrasounds, CTs, and MRIs, as well as other imaging modalities. Radiologists must have a vast knowledge of normal anatomy and pathology, as well as abnormal variants, being able to distinguish benign and malignant tumors, and many other things. He or she must command the requisite knowledge of pediatrics, OB/GYN, surgery, subspecialties, and even emergency medicine. Our department chairman used this acronym, "Charlie–MINT." This stood for the terms "Congenital, Metabolic, Inflammatory, Neoplastic or Traumatic." The best radiologists I know are well-versed in all these areas, and in my view, there is much more to imaging than just scientific knowledge. A truly great radiologist must also rely on intuition, and at times, might even reach out to God for divine inspiration. After all, He is the great Physician. I can't tell you the number of times when I was puzzled with a case while on call and prayed that God would show me the correct diagnosis. And He did!

I wound up getting experience and training with a whole host of attending physicians. Most of these were fair and reasonable doctors with a few exceptions. The most flagrant had to be our neuroradiology professor who happened to be from England and was rather old school and somewhat rigid. This man, while small in stature, was so rough and tough that he would swim in the Pacific Ocean almost every day. Regular folks would not enter the water because it was so cold. At least once a week, the residents would gather in his classroom to review cases, in preparation for the oral board exam.

CHAPTER 9

Imagine standing in front of your peers in a dark class and the x-rays are placed before you. Now it's your time to either sink or swim. After a few seconds of review, he had you repeat the phrase "The gross abnormality on the x-rays is..." Many of the residents would get nervous and subsequently miss the main finding. The humiliation continued, as he had you say, "The other gross abnormality that I missed was..." He was even known to get so exasperated with a couple of residents that he made a few of them sit in the corner of the room wearing a dunce cap. You can't make this stuff up. However, as I got to know him better, I realized that his behavior was sort of an act. He had a most unusual sense of humor for sure. He would only address me by my last name and crucified the pronunciation by calling me Linkofsky. Later that year, I was involved with a most unusual case involving a rare bony overgrowth in the spine. It impinged upon the spinal cord of the patient, requiring surgical decompression and removal. He challenged me to write up that case report with him. I gladly accepted the challenge, and that became the first medical paper that I ever had published as lead author.

I enjoyed researching and writing that article so much, that I ended up participating in writing a few more articles during my fellowship years. I gained a healthy respect for what it takes to get an article published in a credible medical journal.

The Best Laid Plans

Lynn and I had separated for approximately two years right after medical school. God unexpectedly brought us back together. We had a joyful reunion and after a time we decided to get married. So here we were in the fall of 1983. I was deeply involved with my career having finished my written boards and was beginning the preparation for my oral board examination which would be in early June in Louisville, Kentucky. Both of us really wanted to get married in the fall so I devised this scheme that I thought was absolutely brilliant. I was scheduled to be back in the Northeast attending the Armed Forces Institute of Pathology training course in Washington DC. I arranged our honeymoon to be in Bermuda, while simultaneously "attending" a radiology conference during that week. I would use conference time as my leave instead of taking the limited vacation time that I had. As an additional bonus, I could even deduct part of the trip as a business expense. Of course, this was less than honest, but as we all know, desperate people do desperate things. After a spectacular upstate New York

CHAPTER 9

wedding, we headed to Bermuda for our honeymoon as newlyweds.

This combined trip derailed at every level. First off, the hotel was highly mediocre, and the service was suboptimal. I felt convicted as I signed in at the conference and then exited without being seen, so much so that my mind was so preoccupied that I was hardly available for my wife to enjoy our honeymoon. Lynn rightfully scolded me, however, that just added to our collective misery.

Undoubtedly, this was the wrong way to have a honeymoon and start a marriage. I cannot go back in time to rectify that, but I have learned what the most important things in life are. It remains critical to put first things first. Relationships are much more important than careers. At the end of your life, you will be remembered for who you were, not what you did. Leaving a legacy of love is so much more important than reaching career, goals, fame, and even fortune.

If You're Going to San Francisco

Towards the end of my residency, I felt I needed more training in radiology. At that time huge advances were being made in CT and ultrasound; MRI was still in its infancy.

RADIOLOGY, RESIDENCY, AND FELLOWSHIP

I was driven to become the best I could be, and as it turned out I landed a fellowship in CT and ultrasound at one of the country's top medical centers in San Francisco. In mid-1984, Lynn and I embarked on our new adventure to San Francisco to begin my fellowship training. I learned so much during these years and received additional fellowship training in MRI. Lynn worked full-time as a general practitioner across the bridge in Oakland.

Living in the city in the mid-1980s was absolutely amazing. We rented a flat in Twin Peaks and from our balcony we had a panoramic view of the beautiful City by the Bay. There is that saying by an unknown author, sometimes attributed to Mark Twain, which states, "The coldest winter I ever spent was a summer in San Francisco."

One of our most memorable times was being visited for a few days by my aunt and uncle from New York. We connected on a very deep level and had so much fun going on the ferry to Sausalito. Lynn wound up buying a pair of beautiful leather pants at a woman's store. Why, I even tried on a pair of them! How goofy is that? My mom and dad also visited us at another time. The husband of one of our friends was a pilot and flew us in a small plane down to Baja Mexico, to a small fishing village. Dad, Lynn, and I went fishing for mahi-mahi in the Gulf of Mexico with a guide and we hit into a school of them big time. There is

CHAPTER 9

nothing like having a fresh fish dinner under a thatched hut in a very small Mexican town. As we were leaving Baja, things got more than a little dicey, as there was a small problem with the plane. We were never really that worried because the men who were guarding us had submachine guns.

Toward the end of my fellowship years, I was recruited to join a large radiology group in a large community hospital setting in Fresno, California. To me it seemed like a match made in heaven, a dream come true. Have you ever felt that way about a job as you were about to start? Surprisingly, it wound up being like Steve Martin in *Father of the Bride, Part 2*. "All those who think they have it made take one step forward—not so fast George Banks."

CHAPTER 10
LOVE AND MARRIAGE- A LOOK AT OUR LOVE STORY

Having recently graduated with a BS in biology from Manhattan College during the summer of 1976, then July arrived and there was still no word on acceptance to any medical school. Finally, a letter from New York Medical College arrived and I was trembling as I cautiously opened the letter to see what my future held. Would I go on to become a doctor or would I working on the railroad continue for the time being. I had no backup plan at that time. The first word in the letter was congratulations! That acceptance letter totally rocked my world and dramatically changed my whole life's trajectory. I was ecstatic and over the moon with joy. My heart's desire has just come true, and I had only a month to prepare.

There She Was...

I remember the first day of medical school like it was yesterday. Here I was standing in the cafeteria meeting new

CHAPTER 10

classmates. All of a sudden, this beautiful petite young blonde caught my eye. She walked right up to me and said hello. Until then I had only been on a few casual dates and was bound and determined to follow the teachings of my revered anatomy professor. One of his quotes was, "Women and medical school don't mix." I was quite shy around women at that time. She resembled a girl that I knew in college, so I asked her if her name was Brigette. No, her name was Lynn. That was one of my many awkward moments around the opposite sex but fortunately it did not leave a lasting impression with her.

Study Overload and Half a Sandwich

Comparing the rigors of medical school to those of college was like comparing college to high school. We were in classes and labs all day and at night there was a voluminous information overload that each student had to digest. Hours upon hours of study were spent by each of us to learn and memorize important information that would serve as a foundation to becoming a physician. Essentially, we were learning the language of medicine.

    I spent my first month of school living at home and commuting to the Valhalla campus. After the first week, it became apparent that things were just too chaotic for me to live at home. Dad was still drinking heavily and often there was bickering and arguments. I would sleep for a few hours in the early evening when everyone else was still awake., would awaken around 11:00 PM and study for a few hours into the wee hours of the morning, only to catch a couple of more hours of sleep before sunrise. Almost every night and on weekends, I would drive back to campus, a safe haven where I could really concentrate and study.

Each student had a study module, and I would often bring a big sandwich from the deli. As I passed through Lynn's classroom and her study module, I would often see her with her head buried in her books. One day I gathered my courage and asked her if she had eaten recently. She admitted that she had not and was quite hungry, so I gave her half of my sandwich. Then off I went on my way. Awkward!

I also remember times in anatomy lab when I was with a group of male students, and Lynn was nearby with a group of female students. I always had my nose buried in my anatomy book, as the group was dissecting our cadaver, and sometimes Lynn would come over to our table to chat. I presumed that she came over to flirt with the fellows in my group, but I was dead wrong. I found out later that she actually wanted was to see me and gain my attention.

CHAPTER 10

New Meaning for "Hook, Line, and Sinker"

Finally in November I got up the courage to ask Lynn out on a date. Some fellows might take his first date to a nice restaurant and a movie or something along those lines. What not to do on your first date is to bring your girlfriend home to meet and have dinner with your parents, which is precisely what I did. In retrospect, I believe I was so excited that Lynn would be my date that I wanted my parents to meet her. For sure if I could reverse the clock, that's one thing I would have done differently. Overall, the dinner and visit went OK that day. I also took Lynn for a nice stroll around Glenn Island, New Rochelle, where I had many fond memories of fishing with my dad and brothers.

One evening later that month when I dropped Lynn off outside her apartment, we had our first kiss. I fell in love with her, hook, line, and sinker. We became each other's first love and to this day, Lynn remains my one true love. Our developing romance and medical school challenges brought us together and we soon became a team.

Times were really tough, and money was tight. I left home and for short periods of time migrated to different places to study and sleep. The following spring I ended up renting a room with a few other classmates in a large home in Tarrytown, New York. Lynn and I shared some nights at her apartment or in my room and eventually moved in together into an upstairs apartment in a small private home in Mount Vernon which was owned by an old English couple. We stretched the truth by a few years, and told them that we were a married couple, and although it was not true at that time, I think we both knew that we would be married not four years later.

A Time Apart

Towards the end of medical school, our romantic relationship hit a rough patch. As I look back on that time, that is not at all surprising, considering both of our family backgrounds and our levels of emotional and spiritual maturity. Lynn's plan was to move to San Diego to do her internship and begin to fulfill her commitment to the Navy. The navy had awarded her a scholarship to attend medical school; now it was time to fulfill her part of the agreement. We each concurred that some time apart might do us some good. During that same time frame, I had rotated through the core curricula, as well as got some exposure to several different specialties. Up till then I had not found what area I wanted to pursue. Our class had a few lectures from this bright and charismatic radiology professor, and I had an *aha* moment! As if by divine

CHAPTER 10

inspiration I knew in my heart that I wanted to become a diagnostic radiologist. On top of this, I found out that he was relocating to Orange County, California, to become chairman of that radiology department and residency.

My One and Only

I thought it could be a great adventure to live in California for a few years, if I was accepted into that residency. It was an additional bonus to be in proximity to Lynn, should we choose to get back together. I applied and was accepted into that program, but first I had to do my year of internship where I had been matched to a program in Philadelphia. During that year of separation, we each dated other people. God was showing me that while it was enjoyable to date other women, Lynn was truly my one and only. Eventually I moved out to California and God brought us back together. I don't exactly remember who called who, but initially we simply met as old friends. Soon we both realized we were meant for each other and rekindled our love. Lynn picked an idyllic spot in upstate New York that was within driving distance of both sides of our family. We got married in October 1983 in a small church in Cooperstown, New York, called the Farmers' Museum Church. The church was over 200 years old and did not even have electricity. When Lynn arrived at the church, she was greeted with news that the organ had malfunctioned so she decided right on the spot to sing the Lord's Prayer a cappella and informed her sister that she would be singing with her. With no preparation or rehearsal, they sang it pitch perfect! We even had a trumpet solo voluntary performed by one of the finest trumpet players in the northeast. As we lit the candles, her candle fell to the floor. The crowd gasped but Lynn immediately quipped "anything to break up the tension." This drew a round of laughter and appreciation from the congregation. That was over 40 years ago, and boy, the time sure went by fast. Neither of us had any idea what God had planned for us.

Love is Sacrifice

Looking back from this stage and age of life, Lynn and I have lived together through many difficult things here on earth. While medicine remains a very demanding mistress, being a doctor is what I did for my career. Life itself is so much more than that. I have learned is that love is so much more than just saying, "I love you." Love is sacrifice. One of the most important things in life for me has been gradually learning to love more unconditionally.

CHAPTER 10

It took me quite a while and many years of therapy and introspection to be able to separate my medical career from my personal life. Those who focus solely on their career stand a good chance of losing their marriage and families. Reaching out to God can help direct your path to having a harmonious balance in life. While I don't have it entirely together, I consider myself a work in progress. Thank God we can all continue to learn and grow regardless of our age. I have found great comfort spending time with my own daily prayer as well as doing daily morning devotionals with Lynn.

CHAPTER 11
ALL THAT GLITTERS

The spring of 1987 became quite eventful for us. I was winding down my fellowship training when I was recruited by a dynamic radiologist who was the chief of a large and thriving community hospital practice group in Fresno. Lynn and I traveled to Fresno, and we were taken to dinner to meet the group members and their wives. At that time, I was quite naïve and had no idea what I was getting into. Maybe it's best not to know what the future holds as only God really knows the beginning from the end. The job offer seemed almost too good to be true. Everyone seemed so friendly, and the compensation was quite attractive. Fresno itself is in California's Central Valley, a rather dry, semi-arid climate, which is ideal for farming. While it may not be one of the prime California vacation destinations, it has much to offer as a professional community. Day-to-day living expenses are much lower than in many other areas of California, and

CHAPTER 11

the day-to-day moving is a lot easier than in any of the major cities. Still, it took some convincing on my part for Lynn to say yes; however, in the early summer we moved from San Francisco to the Central Valley. We bought a home in town, and right after we moved in, I began what I believed to be my forever job. Everything seemed to be falling into place. I thought I was at the top of my game, having trained in the university environment and having a wide and deep level of knowledge about radiology.

Gulping From the Hose

What I didn't expect was the fast pace and pitch of the caseload. I soon discovered what the day-to-day practice was like for a radiologist in a large community hospital setting. Each radiologist customarily interpreted a high volume of cases. I had interpreted a set number of cases per day in my recent fellowship days, which were only a small fraction of what they were expecting me to do. I felt like Lucille Ball on the assembly line at the chocolate factory. She couldn't handle the pressure, and neither could I. To me, it was like trying to take a gulp of water from a fire hose. Being a perfectionist would not allow me to go at a faster pace than what I felt comfortable with. The struggle within became a daily reality, and my response was increased anxiety.

Where Did the Time Go?

While I did make some strides in my productivity, as time went by it became increasingly apparent to me and to the members of my group that things weren't working out as everyone, including me, had thought they would. I was more what they called an "armchair radiologist" who enjoyed diving into a complex case with my cross-sectional training knowledge, where I could arrive at a differential diagnosis or the precise diagnosis. Time didn't seem to matter during my fellowship, but it sure mattered now! On top of that, there was additional on-call duty about once a week where we would take calls from home. All it took was one or two calls in the middle of the night, and the whole night's sleep would be shot! Those days pre-dated tele-radiology, so when you were called, you were mandated to go to the hospital and take care of whatever it was you were called to do. Sleep deprivation began to steal my joy. Many times, I had to work half day the following day, pushing through under sheer exhaustion. I also had the responsibility of performing certain procedures which were out of my comfort zone, but I must admit I became pretty darn good at doing them.

Finally, as the three-year mark to determine my entrance into full partnership was approaching, the chief

CHAPTER 11

of radiology called a meeting with me. I knew in my heart what he would talk about. I distinctly remember that day before we were scheduled to meet, I read and reread Psalm 23 and 27 and prayed with Lynn. When he informed me that the group voted not to make me a partner, I immediately felt a huge sigh of relief wash over me. It reminded me of the old Alka-Seltzer commercial, plop, plop, fizz, fizz. We all knew that me becoming a partner in that group was not going to work, like trying to fit a square peg in a round hole. Now there was an opportunity to fail forward and find a practice where my style of radiology would fit and would benefit all.

One potentially costly mistake that I made early in my career and marriage was placing more emphasis and importance on my developing career than on my marriage. Through the years Lynn and I had multiple challenges in our relationship. From the get-go my mother took an immediate dislike to Lynn, and Lynn's mom cautioned her not to marry me. What a delight to prove them both wrong. As the years went by, my mom became very fond of Lynn, and sometimes it seemed like Mom preferred her over me. Lynn's mom grew to love and respect me over time, and Lynn told me she never uttered a bad word about me once she got to know me. We both fulfilled our vow to honor and love our parents through to eternity.

We were blessed to have been able to help them both out financially from time to time. What a joy to be able to give back to those who gave so much while raising us.

Make no mistake about it, both our families of origin were quite dysfunctional. My family was a loud and chaotic blue-collar family in Yonkers, New York, like the family in *My Big Fat Greek Wedding* movie. Lynn's family was white collar, educated, and appeared from the outside to be the ideal family. Both our fathers fell victim to the disease of alcoholism, and some might say they carried on the generational curse of alcoholism. As many families do, each of our families blamed the dad for all their problems, and he became the scapegoat. I believe that parental love and support were in short supply when they were raised and that just continued as they raised their children, namely us.

Facing–and Overcoming–Pain

Not long after we got married, I began to realize that I lived with a great deal of emotional and spiritual pain from my upbringing and background. This led me on a wide and deep search and eventually I wound up in long-term psychotherapy. My therapist helped me peel back the layers of my life, working through my anger

CHAPTER 11

and underlying sorrow. I grieved the loss of not having adequate loving and caring parents, and that pain was overwhelming at times. I was eventually able to forgive my parents and others who harmed me, and I more clearly established my roles as husband, father-to-be, family member, Christian and physician. My spiritual journey was also very important. Praying in solitude, and in unison with Lynn, and reaching out to God became increasingly more important. I became the kind of father that my future children deserved to have. For that matter, I consider both Lynn and myself to be generational change agents. That is undoubtedly one of my greatest achievements in life. I am so grateful to have pursued this path, as it helped mold me into the man I am today. Know that even with two strikes against you, you too can still be that overcomer. Having gone through individual and couples therapy, my hope is that couples who plan to have a long-term relationship invest in individual and or couples counseling to address issues before they arise. When you include God in the process, life becomes so much more meaningful.

CHAPTER 12
CHANGING JOBS AND CHANGING DIAPERS

The year was 1990, and not just any ordinary year, but a year filled with profound changes. I experienced a roller coaster of emotions that year. Far and away, the mountaintop experience happened in January, just three days before my birthday. Lynn and I had both participated in the birthing classes and I had convinced myself that I was prepared for the arrival of our first child. I watched with awe and amazement as our beautiful baby girl was born. It took me about three minutes to fall in love with that baby girl. I wanted to always hold her and protect her and keep her happy and healthy. I am convinced that this is the kind of love only parents can feel for their children. This joy could only come from God. I was ecstatic when the nurse announced the baby's weight, six pounds and 14 ounces, or as she phrased it in her thick British accent—6/14! Lynn was absolutely radiant, filled with joy and peace and began breastfeeding right from the start. The nurses instructed me

CHAPTER 12

how to hold our baby and helped me give her the first bath. In my opinion, she was the most beautiful baby ever born with long eyelashes and long piano fingers. My mother-in-law Jane helped us out tremendously for the first couple of weeks. How you best learn to become a good parent is still mysterious to me. My best advice is to learn from other parents, the pediatrics team, books and videos, but know you will largely learn simply by doing and living the experience. Both of us were ushered into a season of chronic sleep deprivation. Lynn, bless her heart, was up and down like a revolving door almost every night. I did my duty when called on to help with diaper changes and whatever else I was assigned. When spring rolled around, we were well integrated into our small SALT (sharing and learning together) Bible study group. As it turned out, another couple in our group had a baby boy at approximately the same time. We shared each other's joys and miseries, as our babies became toddlers and young children.

My focus was now directed toward being a good husband and taking care of our young family. It was a true blessing a few months later when I was informed that I was not going to be made a partner in that community hospital group. What a sigh of relief to have that burden lifted off my shoulders. The group gave me ample time to explore other job possibilities and provided me with good recommendations. As it turns out, we parted on friendly and amicable terms.

First God, Then Family, Then Career

It was becoming increasingly clear to me that God and family were bringing so much more joy than my career ever did. I was embracing family and relationships ahead of my career advancement, and a more Godly balance was in the works. It just so happened that a well-known and respected HMO was new to our town in its early development stages. They were searching for a radiologist with my credentials for an outpatient job, 9:00 a.m. to 5:00 p.m., Monday through Friday. An additional bonus was no weekend work nor on-call responsibilities. Fancy that! The interview went well, and I was hired.

I was blessed to take a few weeks off between jobs, and to go on a trip to New York with my family to be in my brother's wedding. When we returned, I began my new professional endeavor. At first, there were just two radiologists, me and the senior partner. This fellow excelled at producing a high volume of work per unit time. He was especially proficient in x-ray diagnosis and performing small procedures. I had free reign to use my artistic creativity and knowledge in complex cross-sectional imaging.

CHAPTER 12

I felt so fulfilled as I was quite instrumental in raising the standard of care that our institution delivered with ultrasound. I helped train and inspire one of the best ultrasound technologists that I have ever seen in my entire life. She went on to become a pillar in that department for many years. I also enhanced our CT program and began our MRI imaging program from the ground floor. You know that song by Mary Hopkin, "those were the days my friend..."? The five years that I spent at our old clinic doing outpatient radiology were, without a doubt, the most enjoyable years of my entire radiology career. Our HMO was exponentially increasing in membership, and we added two more radiologists. Both fellows have since become my lifelong friends. I remain grateful for those precious years. The truth of the matter is that those years are locked in my memory as among the most enjoyable ever. They were about to fade into the sunset as our brand-new hospital was about to open with an emergency department and inpatient hospital beds, along with mandatory night call and weekend duties. Fast forward to today. Now I look back and thank God for helping me navigate those years as well as many subsequent tougher years, bringing me to the station of life that I am now enjoying.

CHAPTER 13
DAVID AND THE EARLY YEARS

Lynn and I were over the moon in spring of 1992 when we learned she was pregnant with our second child, a boy. Sadly, Lynn's father passed away unexpectedly in the late spring just before he could hear that wonderful news. Everything went as planned until the actual delivery date. Suddenly, during labor, the baby's heart rate decelerated to such a dangerously low level that her OB began sharpening his scalpel intending to do a stat C-section. When Lynn heard what he was going to do, she went into mama mode and quickly delivered David spontaneously. Just in the nick of time. What an amazing blessing to have another beautiful baby! My mother-in-law Jane, also a nurse, was again present at the delivery, and was among the first people to hold David. Something happened, or I should say didn't happen, right then which we were not to discover until many years later. To her shock and surprise, David never made eye contact with her. In her experience

CHAPTER 13

Many of the babies she helped deliver did make eye contact immediately after birth. She knew deep in her heart that something wasn't quite right but never divulged this to us. I believe she just loved us too much to raise any sort of red flag.

The Stress of a Newborn

Lynn and I were ecstatic to have a New Year's baby. We both believed that David was quite healthy except for him needing to be under a photo light for a short period of time because of jaundice. A more ominous problem eventually surfaced during breastfeeding. Our first child breast-fed with no significant problems, but it was extremely difficult for David to latch on to Lynn's breast despite the expert help of lactation experts. There were many sleepless nights, lots of tears mutually shared. Over time we learned that David had a very poor sucking ability, coupled with a terrible case of colic. Still, we trudged on with family life and my job at the facility. Shortly before David's birth, Lynn had to play hardball with management to get much needed maternity leave—a mere 20 days. How generous! At this time in history, the average maternity leave is approximately 10 weeks and could be extended to 12 weeks with the family medical leave act

(FMLA). Why, some men even get up to two months for paternity leave, imagine that!

Something's Wrong

By now, Lynn's sister, also a physician, began raising questions about David and his decreased muscle tone. He still wasn't making eye contact. We both remained in denial, believing (and hoping) that she was exaggerating. Lynn returned home from a weekend with her family with a worried look on her face, and some fear that something was wrong with her precious son. She insisted that we take David in for an urgent care visit to make sure he was OK. That date was April 26th, 1993, and is etched in my mind forever. We were in the pediatrics examining room, proud parents, but with a vague uneasy feeling that something may be wrong with David. We desperately wanted the doctor's assurance that all was well. We watched as he performed the usual physical exam and saw his facial expression change from serene and confident to a solemn stare, almost like he had seen a ghost. The look on his face shot terror through both our hearts. Our denial got ripped away when he told us he was really concerned about David. He mentioned the term developmental delay.

CHAPTER 13

Little did we know that in the coming weeks and months we would become very familiar with that term. Other difficult medical terms also became part of our usual vocabulary when speaking about David. In rapid sequence, David got an urgent CT of his head, a pediatric neurology consult, and subsequently an EEG and MRI.

Our World Shifted

In one fell swoop, our entire world was turned upside down! The MRI revealed a dysmyelination pattern in his brain. Both of us being physicians made this news seem even worse. I quickly consulted a world-famous pediatric neuroradiologist whom I knew from my days of fellowship training. He thought this was probably an inborn error of metabolism which led to the myelin sheath being abnormal, delayed, or arrested in its maturation. The substance myelin facilitates conduction of signals within the brain and spinal cord. Abnormalities within the myelin sheath can cause all sorts of horrendous problems including lack of sensation, movement, and even cognition, depending on which nerves are involved. Mere words cannot tell you how often we cried as we struggled through some of the first stages of grief, suffering along with David. For me, this was among one of the most painful experiences I ever endured.

Just when we thought it couldn't get any worse, the other shoe dropped. Seizures stormed into David's life when he was approximately seven months old. The first seizure terrified us, and we immediately took him to pediatric urgent care. Right after his cursory exam, that doctor, who was also a colleague, turned to us in a condescending and demeaning manner and said, "Don't you know your son has cerebral palsy? If you haven't seen the movie *Lorenzo's Oil*, you need to see it soon."

I was shocked at his businesslike and dispassionate proclamation. Lynn became so angry that she verbally tore him up one side and down the other, and as near as I can remember, he was still backpedaling when we left the room. David had tonic clonic seizures, or infantile spasms, which were very poorly controlled with the medication regimens available at that time in the 90s. I recall counting 142 seizures in one day, and those were just the ones that I witnessed. There were probably many more than that which were below the threshold of our recognition. We did anything and everything we could to prevent the situation known as *status epilepticus*, which basically is continual seizure activity which, if not broken, can be fatal. Treatment included benzodiazepines such as oral Ativan. The pharmacist created a specialty concoction of liquid valium to be inserted rectally in dire situations. Nevertheless, a few times the seizures could not be broken and necessitated emergency hospitalizations and admission into the neonatal ICU. The more seizures that David had, the further delayed his development would become, causing him to miss developmental milestones. Our hope was fading away along with David's delayed development.

The Third Strike

Lastly there were the visits with the metabolic geneticist. After his thoroughly examining David then getting all the tests results, we arrived for the follow-up visit. These were his words: "David is never going to walk, talk, or ride a bicycle. I'll bet you are familiar with the old baseball phrase, one, two, three strikes, you're out." The third strike came a year or two later when another of my colleagues, a professed Christian no less, refused to approve a request for additional treatment for our son. David was not improving at an acceptable rate to merit the treatment. He went on to tell us that David was the third most expensive pediatric patient that our organization had in the entire area. That was the last straw.

Time to Man Up...Both of Us

Neither Lynn nor I accepted these words and advice as the final word. One thing about Lynn and me is that we both grew up in New York, and when the going gets tough, the tough get going. We decided those pediatricians were no longer fit to be on our team and my job was to give them the boot. In other words, you're fired! This action went against who I was as a people pleaser, but the gloves were off, and it was time for me to man up. I did just that. We went forward and no longer allowed any dream stealers to be on our team. Over time we picked an amazing team of doctors, therapists, special ed teachers, and aides who were competent yet empathic, and who shared our vision of bringing the best care possible to David. The love and caring that they demonstrated went far beyond their job descriptions; it was truly their mission in life. We welcomed these Godly people into our lives and allowed all of us to be ministered to by their caring and empathic attitudes. They were almost like angels among us.

If you or a family member happen to have a disability, have you ever felt like certain doctors just didn't treat you with respect or may have given you substandard care? I recently perused an article regarding physician attitudes about caring for people with disabilities.

CHAPTER 13

In one study, several focus groups of doctors who were protected by anonymity admitted they don't want to see patients with disabilities. Why is that? One certain reason is that disabled patients took up way too much time for that 15-minute time slot. The problem of course is multifactorial and beyond the scope of this book. The study concluded that the culture of medicine needs to change regarding caring for those with disabilities. One final thought–don't take every single word that a doctor utters as gospel truth. If these things happened to us as two medical doctors (and believe me, they did), how is the everyday patient and family being treated? I shudder to think that it could have been even worse looking back. The best advice I have to offer is to gather a medical team who is actually on your side as you go into battle, and in so doing you may be able to snatch victory from the jaws of defeat. We have found great benefit from having God on our team. You may not win the battle, but you will win the war. The ending may or may not be what you wanted but will be that which God desires.

CHAPTER 14
"LORD, WE NEED A MIRACLE"

Come along with me, as I painfully revisit the years of David's life. I am certain of one thing: Lynn and I desperately wanted and needed a creative miracle. We needed David to be completely healed and restored. Just imagine, both parents are MDs, and they pull out all the stops, using all their influence and connections to get the very best medical care for him. Despite using every resource available, his condition and our hope went from bad to worse. His seizures were out of control and so were our lives. We even took him all the way up to Vancouver BC Children's Hospital when he was about a year-and-a-half old to consult with a renowned pediatric neurologist. He treated us like we were dignitaries, charging us nothing for his consultation. He even prescribed two seizure medications that were not, yet FDA approved in the United States that decreased the number and severity of those seizures. To me that man was a saint.

CHAPTER 14

Enduring Reality

Here was the stark reality: David, while technically a child, was functionally like a quadriplegic infant, wheelchair-bound, and all. At various times in his life, he had to endure nasogastric tube feedings, and even gastrostomy (G) tubes. Speaking of G-tubes, David had a bad medical complication after placement of one of his G-tubes. Unfortunately, a small portion of his colon had gotten trapped between the stomach and skin surface and was inadvertently perforated. When the tube was revised, David became deathly ill from colonic contents leaking into his abdomen and needed emergency surgery to remove a small portion of his colon. While God saved his life, I had to work through my anger and sadness with that doctor in his office, but God helped me find forgiveness. We moved on from there. David was in and out of the children's hospital so frequently that one time I jokingly asked the nurse if we could get frequent flyer miles, ha ha! You know during tragic times humor can be so helpful. Once we had to call 911 in the middle of the night as David was in status epilepticus. Picture firemen marching through the house wearing all their gear, and our kids on the stairway hiding out of fear. David's medical condition was quite fragile, but mercifully, we remained in denial about just how serious it really was. None of us in our primary family came through this unscathed. We were about to discover that God was with us, holding us up every step of the way.

The Church—the Body of Christ

Until David was two years old, we were attending a large Christian community church. We kept him with us during the service for as long as we could. However, David would make unpredictable noises and could easily disturb the congregation and disrupt the church service. I remain eternally grateful for the pastor of that church. Despite his busy schedule and people clamoring for his attention, many Sundays after church, he would gather our family in his office, get down on his knees, and pray for David, and for all of us. Those times are etched in my mind and heart forever. That Pastor channeled God's love right into our hearts, lifting our spirits, and helping us to keep on keeping on.

One day, Lynn was at her workplace when a custodian there (also a pastor) told her about a small inner-city church where he felt we would be welcomed into the congregation. We decided to try it out. One Sunday we got everybody loaded in the van and headed to this

CHAPTER 14

downtown church. This church had mostly Black and Hispanic members, with a few Caucasians sprinkled in. It was full-gospel nondenominational, and in short order became very much like family to us. Pastor Doug and I became very good friends. One day I asked him flat out, how do you figure us being at your church? He replied, "Here at this downtown church we minister to the down-and-outers and the up-and-outers!" I guess if the shoe fits, wear it. That was almost 30 years ago, and Doug and I remain among the best of friends to this day.

At this church there was always plenty of prayer and times when I could feel the presence of God in the room. Lynn and I began making connections regarding healing services at other churches in the community, as well as visiting evangelists who had healing ministries. We even went to a few Catholic charismatic healing services which were absolutely wonderful. Enter a controversial healing evangelist into our lives, Benny Hinn and his miracle crusades. The first miracle crusade that we brought our family to happened to be nearby in Anaheim, California in April '94. My mom and dad were here visiting us during that time. They were such good sports and even went with us to the miracle crusade. They were our allies and in solidarity with us for David's healing although they knew it was likely only a very slim chance. We had a short private meeting with Benny after the crusade when he told us that he felt the anointing of the Holy Spirit and told us expect to see a change. We left there with more hope than when we came. Our desire to persevere and go on was rekindled.

Joni and Friends

Fast forward the clock a couple of years in David's life to when he turned four years old. Somebody connected us with the most amazing Christian disability ministry called Joni and Friends. Their purpose is to accelerate Christian ministry in the disability community. They have a worldwide footprint and present the hope of the gospel to people affected by disability through programs and various outreaches. We were so blessed to attend one of their family retreats in 1997. It really opened our eyes to see how many families are affected by disability. In fact, some of the challenged kids and adults appeared to be a lot worse off than David, and by comparison, I believed we had it good. We always returned home with renewed hope and invigorated.

CHAPTER 14

Witnessing Miracles

Would you like to know about some of the different miracles we witnessed? One of them had to do with a change of heart from the physician in chief at my facility. Along the way, one of the pediatricians told us that David was blind, and essentially couldn't see. He had a bad case of strabismus. It just so happened that a renowned pediatric ophthalmologist who specialized in strabismus surgery was working in our town for about one month while our regular pediatric ophthalmologist was on leave. My request to the director to have this specialist operate on David's eyes was initially refused. However, after I pleaded David's case in earnest, he reversed that decision and approved the surgery. The surgery went well, and the surgeon reported there was a perfect result. Now David could see! His prescription called for thick lenses which enabled him to see even better. How well he really could see God only knows (and He does!).

A couple of the specialists who saw David early on stated he would not be able to eat solid foods, but he was able to eat solids for a few years. For a couple of years David was also able to use a tristander device to be able to stand with assistance. Pastor Doug became our advocate and attended several the individualized education program (IEP) meetings. He became a first-hand witness of God's miraculous intervention on David's behalf. David developed more and more of an emotional range and could smile and laugh as he became more cognitively aware. He responded more and more and more as time went on and was eventually able to visually track people and objects. Doug relayed how the IEP team, while very professional, were also very collaborative. They caught our hopes and dreams and lined up with our vision for David. All I can say is that God was truly present and did miraculous interventions on David's behalf for everyone in his circle to witness; all for God's honor and glory. Many people would be drawn to David as if there was an aura about him. Maybe in the spiritual realm, he was even wearing a halo.

We Got What We Came For

2001 was a very eventful year. We attended our second JAF family retreat. We also attended a Benny Hinn miracle crusade that summer. The indoor stadium held between 15-20,000 people, packed to capacity. Our family was invited to go on stage in front of the entire audience. With cameras rolling and thousands of eyes on us, Benny came up to us and asked me why we were here and what I

CHAPTER 14

would like God to do. To my recollection, I responded, "I would love to see David healed, and for him to be able to walk and talk about the glory of what God has done in his life." He then quickly turned to the audience and exhorted them to stand up, whoever could, and then he said a very touching prayer. While I can't remember the words, I was so caught up in the moment that didn't even realize what was going on in that large audience. A few days after the crusade, a medical staff worker unexpectedly came to visit me at my office while I was at work. She said she saw me over the weekend, and I knew immediately that she had been at that event. I then asked her what her experience from her perspective was. She replied that during that prayer, she personally witnessed a number of people falling back in their chairs. Some people would describe that as being slain in the spirit. For me, it was feeling God's presence with overwhelming love and hope. When we got back to our seats our in-laws expressed their disappointment that David hadn't been healed. While that was true, my immediate response to them was, "we got what we came here for." The miracle that I received was that of perseverance and increased strength to keep on keeping on.

"LORD, WE NEED A MIRACLE"

Sinking in Quicksand

The last few months of David's life in 2002 were terrible for all of us, especially David. Until then we had a full-time live-in nanny who had also learned the nursing skills needed for caring for David. After a falling out, she was dismissed. That was a huge curveball, which threw our lives way out of balance, as it was now up to Lynn and me to be the sole caretakers of David. His care truly was 24/7. Not only was there a rigorous G-tube feeding schedule, but he also received multiple medications daily as well as diaper changes. We were always on alert monitoring and treating seizures. Trying to work half time on top of that was virtually impossible. Our family was sinking in quicksand. How could we best care for David? Through the disability community, we found out about a very reputable group home about a mile from our home where they had skilled staff 24/7, who took excellent care of severely disabled kids like David. It seemed like a match made in heaven. Close to home, easy to visit, and quality care—everyone in our family would benefit, especially David. To me, one of the best things in life is creating win-win situations.

CHAPTER 14

Overdue Respite

As it turns out, Lynn and I took a long, much needed, and overdue getaway to the east coast. This was the first time in several years the two of us were going away. Just five days after placing David in the home, we flew east to begin a short vacation. David was all settled in the group home and our kids were at home with a trusted babysitter. We had no idea what was just around the corner.

We were fast asleep the following morning, when the chilling phone call came in at 6:00 a.m. It was the director of David's group home. My first thought was that he was calling simply to follow up with us, but that wasn't the case. He had been checked by staff at around 4:00 a.m. and was resting comfortably. Just a short time later during another check, his breathing stopped and he was unresponsive. CPR was immediately started and 911 was immediately called. Despite their best efforts, the paramedics were unable to revive David.

The director tearfully told me that David had died. I just stared at the phone totally stunned. Lynn turned to me and wailed as only a mother can. We both just cried. *How could David possibly be found unresponsive by a staff person and why couldn't he be resuscitated?* This seemed meaningless and unreal. Later we were told that the night before he died, David had stayed up almost all night, silent and gazing around as if he was engaged in some sort of silent dialogue—maybe with God? I'll just have to wait until the other side of eternity to find out the answer to that one.

Holding on to Faith

Right now, I will digress back a few months before David passed. This has to do with my experience with a certain "faith healer." This professed healing evangelist was in town for a special event which, in this case involved making money. In his message, he claimed that God worked through him to raise a man up from the dead. Shortly after his message, he singled me out and prophesied that God told him that if I just prayed and fasted, that God would completely raise David up and heal him completely. After I told Pastor Doug about this proclamation, he wanted to take this fellow out to the woodshed.

Now it just so turned out that the day that David died, this fellow was back in town. Lynn knew this from a mutual friend, and she begged me to let them go to the morgue to see if God would work his magic and raise David up from the dead. Understanding that dead is dead, I still gave Lynn the go-ahead as I could sense the

CHAPTER 14

desperation she felt. Amazingly, she convinced the clinical coordinator to allow him to visit the morgue. This fellow prayed for a raising from the dead, like Lazarus. As it turns out, his later comment was that David's face was so serene that he knew that he went home into the arms of a loving God. A couple of ways to know a true prophecy is if it lines up with the Scriptures, and if that prophecy comes to pass. It was a bitter lesson for me to learn but going forward I have a better knowledge of discerning false prophecies.

That Others May Benefit

Later that morning, I received a call from someone at the organ donor bank. She expressed her condolences, and respectfully requested permission to harvest the corneas from David's eyes and whatever heart valves from his heart that could help patients going forward. My first response was (hell) no! As Lynn and I walked and talked, we both soon realized that David's organs could continue to help the living. I believe that at that point, God touched our hearts. David would have wanted it that way. I called her back with a definitive yes.

Final Arrangements

Lynn and I walked, talked, and cried throughout the day. That night we toasted David, drank wine, and laughed and cried over dinner. The following day we returned to California and were met at the airport terminal by Pastor Doug. Breaking the news of David's death to our other children was one of the most painful things I have ever had to do. All of us had lots and lots of tears. The following day, Doug went with us to the funeral home, helping us pick out a casket and to get a fair and square deal to use their chapel facility for David's memorial service.

The Reflection of God

David's memorial service was a celebration, a homegoing. The chapel was packed with people from all walks of life. Many of my colleagues of all different faiths and backgrounds attended. One of my colleagues told me that he felt like this was more like an altar call. When I spoke at the service, I mentioned that while David never said a word, he spoke volumes into the hearts of all who knew him. While it was true, that he never walked, he walked intimately with God. He brought us so much joy and laughter and love that we are more fully human because

CHAPTER 14

of David. There were times in David's life when someone would come up to him to visit and I would just tell them, "If you look carefully into his eyes, you can actually see God's reflection." David has no more pain, no more suffering or procedures or seizures or hospitalizations. God took him home to his eternal reward totally whole and completely healed. O Lord, remember, David, and all the hardships he endured" (Psalm 132:1).

Do I still believe in miracles? Absolutely! God set David free from his earthly body and saved him from further episodes of pain and suffering. God blessed us with David for the time we had, and we are each more empathic and loving and more fully human from this bitter-sweet experience. Lynn and I are among the minority; those whose marriages survived having had a very medically challenged child. And through it all I am amazed every day at the wonderful people that my children have become. Thank you, God, for having a blessed us with David's life. My belief is that God performs miracles for His honor and glory and His perfect timing. Yes, some miracles happen instantaneously, yet others happen over time. When you accept Jesus as your Lord and Savior you gain eternal salvation and a heavenly reward when you die. That is the greatest miracle of all, being called to faith and given the gift of life. God remains waiting for you, all you have to do is ask.

CHAPTER 15
SAMMY THE HAMMY

The year was 1997 and we were both 43 years old. At that time, our primary family unit included a seriously disabled four-year-old son and a healthy older daughter. Most couples would have called it quits, at least as far as having more children. Or maybe they would have called quits on their marriage as over 80% of marriages who have a disabled child end in separation or divorce. Beyond those factors, David's medical geneticist warned us that if we had another boy, there could easily be a chance that he too would be disabled, although there was no definite diagnosis made with David. We realized that his statement was simply an educated guess. But what if his hypothesis was correct?

Here We Go Again

It was late spring when Lynn came home waving the positive pregnancy test at me. We were both overjoyed! At the time I wasn't sure whether we were courageous or just plain crazy. Maybe it was a little bit of both. Sammy entered our lives and joyfully added to our family that September. Lynn graciously gave me the opportunity and privilege to name him, and I felt "inspired" to name him Gregory. Samuel was a traditionally prominent name on Lynn's side of the family, so we chose that for his middle name. Calling him Gregory or Greg, Jr. lasted barely a week when we all realized that somehow, he just looked and acted like a Sammy.

A Drum of His Own

We could tell from the get-go that he was no ordinary child. He truly seemed to dance to the beat of a different drummer almost from day one. A good example comes to mind and happened while we were on a family vacation on Sanibel Island, Florida. Sammy was almost four years old at the time when we went to have dinner at the hotel restaurant which had a live band. Suddenly, we discovered Sammy was missing. Lynn and I lost it with a few moments of sheer panic. Just then a fellow at the nearby table turned to us and said, "Is that your son up on the stage?" We fixed our gaze on the stage where Sam was in all his glory breakdancing to the beat of the music, along with plenty of clapping and cheering from the audience. We again confirmed—this kid was a real live wire!

Elvis Has *Not* Left the Building

One day in second grade one of Sammy's classmates brought in some Elvis Presley memorabilia for the weekly show-and-tell. It was a big hit in class, and his beloved teacher told the class how much she loved Elvis and his music. Right then Sammy decided that he was going to become an Elvis tribute artist (ETA). That weekend, Sam and I went to Costco and bought a couple of packages of Elvis CDs and DVDs. He played them over and over again, and imprinted the style, mannerisms, and to some extent, the voice of a young Elvis. Soon we hand-picked an old rock'n'roll star to be his vocal coach and right before our very eyes, he transitioned into an accomplished ETA. At the age of 10, he performed at a local Italian restaurant where the owner billed him as "Little Baby Elvis." She even had a poster made to herald the event. We made it a grand evening with family and friends, as well as the regular restaurant patrons. We all cheered him on as he performed wearing a white imitation Elvis jumpsuit. He remained so dedicated that Lynn and I decided to get him an authentic replica of a real Elvis outfit. I researched

CHAPTER 15

where one could buy such an outfit and subsequently called the owner of an Elvis Presley specialty store in the Midwest where they custom made him a child's version of the gold lame jacket. She initially refused the request as she warned how much work would be involved in making this, and how much it would cost. I was persistent and steadfast until she finally agreed. Sam wore that jacket at a number of events, the largest of which was performing at his school fundraiser in front of more than 400 people. You had to see it to believe it! Here was our beloved son, hair coiffed, gold lame jacket, Elvis's scarves, guitar, props, and all. And, by God, he was only 11 years old at the time! Elvis never really left the building although that talent was eventually stored up in Sam's armamentarium.

Destined for the Spotlight

Later that year, his vocal coach encouraged him to audition for the children's version of the musical "The Wiz." She believed he was ready to branch out into entertainment and from the audition landed the role of the Tin Man. That was it. He was off to the races with no turning back. Sam ended up as the lead or prominent role in quite the number of shows. He especially liked to portray the eccentric character in a play, such as Lord Farquaad in Shrek. He is the type of individual for whom nearly everything he touches turns to gold. He was in many musicals, did improv, participated in debates and other leadership roles.

Sam had discovered his passion and purpose in life. Destiny was calling him to become a world-class singer, vocal coach, actor, musician, and songwriter. Lynn's side of the family has a rich musical heritage. Her father was a renowned trumpet player in upstate New York, and his dad was the leader of the town's marching band back in the day. Before she switched to premed, Lynn was a music major in college. She sings and plays the piano and guitar and has a lovely voice. My musical claim to fame is that I play a pretty mean accordion. Sam got the generational DNA and has taken his talent to a whole new level. He is simply a bright shining star who lights up the stage.

Whose Dreams Are They Anyway?

Sam is undoubtedly one of the most kind and authentic people I know. One day in his mid-teens, he shared with us that he was gay. I felt like I had been sucker punched in the stomach. Lynn and I both initially felt shock, anger, sadness, and loss. We both felt like we were losing another

CHAPTER 15

son. I believe part of this has to do with the fact that David had passed away when Sam was four. That whole experience Had been a game changer for us. I believe that after this, Lynn and I held onto him extra tightly for fear that we might lose him also. We put a lot of our added hopes and dreams on Sammy. Why of course he would find the right girl, get married, and have a traditional family. But they were just that—our hopes and dreams. We didn't really consider how Sammy felt.

A God of Love

It was time for me to face my own biases and prejudices. Initially, this was quite a painful process. My therapist helped me navigate through and I really became introspective. Gradually through prayer, reflection, and even some of my own research, I arrived at a peaceful place in my own heart, a place of acceptance and affirmation. I am a practicing Christian, and I'll be the first to admit I lead an imperfect life. I continue to strive to be less judgmental and more loving and accepting as I go down the path of my life. The God I know is a God of unconditional love. I have also witnessed firsthand the devastation in Christian families when a gay or lesbian member comes out. I have seen families banish the individual, like excommunication. The Jesus that I know would never have done anything like that. I have also seen families where the couple starts off in a heterosexual marriage, have children, only to later discover that one of them is gay which can create a boatload of problems.

Another part to this is looking at sexuality from Sam's perspective. Together over the years we have opened up a whole new dialogue. The discussions we have had indicate that his journey is not an easy one by any stretch of the imagination. Sam has told me that he did not choose to be gay. There were telltale signs that others picked up in his childhood and early adolescence that I am just learning about. I truly respect him for being authentic and true to himself as well as being honest with all of us.

Sam remains a most unique and talented individual. He has a toolbox full of talent which he is sharing with the world. One of my greatest joys in life is to watch him perform in his various shows and gigs. We are all God's children, and I am very fortunate to have been Sam's biological father. When you get down to it, all of us belong to God, and each one of us has our own unique individual journey in life. I am very proud of Sam and love him with my whole heart. Yes, one facet is that he happens to be gay, but my commitment is to love, support, and encourage him and each of my family members as they travel

CHAPTER 15

their individual journeys in life. Wow, what a relief it is to have the heavy responsibility of judging others lifted off my shoulders! When all is said and done, God is the only judge who matters in life, and in matters beyond life.

CHAPTER 16
GRIN AND BEAR IT... MY EARLY RETIREMENT

Let's crank the clock back to about 12 years ago, when I was 58 years old. Well, actually about five years before that time. Have you ever experimented by trying any type of martial arts, like taekwondo? When young Sammy was about 10 years old, we decided to take up taekwondo together as father and son. At the time, I thought it would be a great way to bond and to appear to be a tough guy in Sammy's eyes. I really enjoyed it at first. Sammy and I both had the ability to kick and punch, and it was quite a good workout. Then one day, quite unexpectedly, in our master bathroom, Sammy decked me with a roundhouse kick to my thigh. As I lay on the floor rubbing my aching thigh, I asked, "Why did you do that?" He just smiled and said, "Dad, I needed to practice that kick." At that time, I remembered what my dear old mom would say—just grin and bear it.

All the students in our group were on a quest for that elusive black belt. We were sharpening our skills and there

CHAPTER 16

was great camaraderie and cohesiveness in our group. One day while I was sparring with a partner I delivered an extra hard kick, and that kick was a game changer for me. I instantly felt something snap deep in my left thigh. From that time on, I had this chronic nagging left hamstring pain. It bothered me so much that I even had an MRI of my thigh, which turned out to be negative. The discomfort persisted and I endured that pain, especially when I played golf. A few years later I was running a bit late for a parents' meeting at Sam's middle school. I was trotting and walking quickly on the huge campus when suddenly out of nowhere both of my legs and feet went numb. I sat down for a few minutes and regained the feeling and sensation back in my legs, but I knew in my heart that something was terribly wrong.

Becoming the Bionic Man

My doctor finally ordered an MRI of my lumbar spine. It turned out that I had severe spinal stenosis in my lower back at the L 4–5 level. In simple terms, a combination of bony and ligamentous overgrowth, along with some forward slippage of the L4 onto the L5 vertebra, created a narrowing of the diameter of my spinal canal. This was analogous to squeezing a water hose and choking off the water supply. This narrowing caused compression of the blood supply to the spinal nerves and created terrible symptoms. The ultimate solution was what my neurosurgeon referred to as "the commando procedure." This involved a lumbar laminectomy, the careful removal of the disc at that level, and fusion of the two adjacent vertebrae. The job would be finished with posterior fixation with 3/8-inch thick titanium rods and screws. I joked that I was going to be the Bionic Man, ha ha!

    I delayed having that surgery for as long as I possibly could. My symptoms eventually affected my performance as a doctor, not to mention how I was doing as a husband and father. It finally got to the point where I couldn't stand it anymore. I had to prove it to myself that I was ready to undergo that type of surgery. Those of us who have had major surgery, know when that time has arrived. Shortly before the surgery I went on partial disability. A very hard part of this whole process was recognizing and accepting the fact that I was truly partially disabled. After all, doctors are supposed to be invincible, aren't they? So here I was, being wheeled into the operating suite and the last thing I remember was my neurosurgeon asking me if I had anything to say before the surgery. I exclaimed, "Git-r-done!" in honor of Larry, the Cable Guy. I was in the operating room for over six hours lying face down. I

CHAPTER 16

had the benefit of the combined efforts of two experienced neurosurgeons working together and they did a careful and meticulous job. Although I have some residual effects from the disease process, I was very grateful to have had that life-changing operation.

Navigating New Territory

I wound up taking a few months of sick leave which gave me precious time to heal, pause, and reevaluate my life. I was finally able to return to work but only part time. It was soon apparent that there was a huge mismatch between return-to-work expectations from administration and my actual abilities to perform my job after the operation. After a couple of very unpleasant interactions with administration and human resources, I sought the help of a life coach to help me navigate my new situation. The fellow with whom I worked was a former CEO of a couple of large companies and had experience working on both sides of the table with human resources. This experience was new territory for me and the first time I ever had to deal with human resources. Life was difficult with my new circumstance of being partially disabled, but I gradually learned how to fight fair and square in the workplace. That last year was truly a battle to make it to the finish line of age 60. That was when I could graduate to full early retirement.

One day a trusted individual in my life finally asked me why I had never applied for long-term partial disability. The truth of the matter initially was that I didn't think I needed it or would qualify for it. However, after pondering that question and discussing it with Lynn and praying about it, I applied. The first application was rejected. I then sought counsel from a Workmen's Compensation attorney, who advised me that I wouldn't qualify for partial disability. It turns out that sometimes professional opinions can be wrong. What he failed to realize that as a New Yorker, I didn't know how to give up; that was just not in my DNA. After much prayer with Lynn and pondering, I reapplied for partial disability, emphasizing the new challenges that I was facing. Almost as if by magic, the company reversed its initial decision, and reversed its initial decision, and declared that yes indeed, I really did qualify for partial disability. There is a lot to be said for persistence, especially when you have a just cause. Never give up or give in.

CHAPTER 16

The Writing on the Wall

The writing on the wall was becoming increasingly clear and all I had to do was to hang on that final year until I reached the age of 60. There were a few special challenges and curveballs that I had to deal with during that last year. As a special pre-retirement present, I had been given a disproportionate amount of the holiday call schedule for the upcoming year. I shared this challenge with the entire group. Being the great colleagues that they were, we ended up being able to balance things out somewhat. But the message to me was crystal clear, it was time to move on.

Crossing the Finish Line

I'll never forget my final day of call. It was a day shift call, the Sunday after Christmas right before New Year's. The finish line was in sight as I was rapidly approaching my 60th birthday. I had received a request to vacate my office by the following Tuesday, which was two days later. However, I was eager to exit stage left, so right after my shift that Sunday, my daughter and future son-in-law arrived with a large SUV. They were a great help for me to empty my office. I've never been so excited before about packing up and leaving. I vowed not to let the door hit me in the rear end on the way out. I felt like I was being liberated. The hardest part was surrendering my ID card, as I could no longer gain special access to visit my doctor friends in the ED.

I still love the field of radiology, and was very blessed to have had a great career. In fact, many people along the way and afterwards have told me that I was one of the best radiologists that they had ever worked with. I believe there was a lot to be said for leaving a career when you're at the top of your game, not after you find yourself on the downslope. God knows I've always strived to perform my very best throughout my career. A variety of factors helped make my entrance into my second act a no brainer—the increasing demands of productivity, increasing complexity of the cases coupled with the onerous on-call schedule, as well as my health-related issues, Now that this chapter of life was ending, what would be next? I was excited to move on to my second half.

CHAPTER 17
MY SECOND ACT

Do you remember Bing Crosby in the movie White Christmas, singing this song about what do you do with a general when he stops being a general? There is a certain similarity in the amount of respect and honor that are usually given to a physician who has the responsibility of caring for patients. Now I was about to say goodbye to my medical career and begin a whole new chapter in my life.

Shifting Gears

I began in earnest to examine my passions and what truly inspired me. Now at age 60, what was it that helped me live my life to the fullest now that my career in diagnostic radiology was fading into the background? Retirement for me became the opportunity to explore some of the possibilities that I had set aside while building my career. I revisited many of the activities that brought me joy and inspiration in the past. For one, I rekindled my love of music and playing the accordion. Then there were those times I got to spend with my daughter while we traveled up and back from San Francisco to choose her magnificent wedding gown. Those times were precious and priceless. I also had more time to devote to both the Christian and secular communities by serving on a couple of different boards of directors. Joni and Friends, as I previously described, was undoubtedly one of my favorites. This organization continues to minister to families with disabilities. It was truly a blessing for me to be able to give back to this worthwhile ministry. It was also a way for me to honor David's memory and to spread God's love to others, as some of the people on the board had a member of their family who had a disability themselves. We were truly helping some of God's most needy children.

Then there was the nonprofit children's musical theater foundation in our central valley town. The climate in the valley would get really hot and dry in the summer, with the air quality at times being smoggy and unhealthy. However, the atmosphere in our community theater was always warm, alive, and healthy with plenty of top-notch entertainment. In fact, a handful of performers from that theater ended up performing on Broadway and on TV and in film. Sammy had grown up performing in this setting,

CHAPTER 17

where he matured as a singer and actor. The best way I could have honored the people who mentored and taught Sammy was to serve on their nonprofit board of directors. My main job was to participate in fundraising so this group could continue to train children from all walks of life in the performing arts. While in this group, the kids learned many valuable life skills, such as honesty, and accountability, as well as how to perform at their personal best. Sammy and I both got to participate on the board together for one year.

Launching Sammy

I was blessed to have been an active participant with Sammy as his amazing story unfolded. His scholastic and performing skills were showcased during his application to multiple colleges and universities. To gain entrance into a top-notch musical theater program, a student first must pass the rigorous academic standards. Then comes the audition, usually a short segment of singing, and at least one or two types of monologues. I was fortunate to accompany Sam to every audition and interview. Interestingly, some auditions proved shallow, only being five or ten minutes in length. UCLA, on the other hand, had a full day filled with interviews and auditions in various modalities. This process of vetting was nearly six hours long, and believe me, they only accepted the top cohort of students. Most of the candidates who were chosen ended up attending and graduating together. Sam had found his bliss at UCLA, where he further matured as an actor, singer, and dancer.

Serving God in the Hospital

A couple of years later I was honored to serve as an assistant to the hospital chaplain at my former hospital. After going through the required training, the chaplain sent me off solo on my weekly assignment to visit a set number of hospitalized patients. I believe God worked through me to bring some comfort to those in distress. Sometimes I offer an encouraging word or said a prayer or two with them. Some people enjoyed having me read a scripture verse or giving them a small booklet or a Bible. I can only imagine what some of my former hospital-based physicians and consultants from all different races and religions thought when they would see me up on the floor. After all, I was one of the radiologists who usually only stayed in our dark rooms downstairs. It was a season where I grew spiritually in my life, and in many ways felt that God led and directed me in this situation, according to His purposes, and I

CHAPTER 17

trusted Him for the outcome. In essence, I surrendered to God and let Him use me as his instrument.

Is There a Psychiatrist in the House?

After I retired Lynn continued to work full-time as a staff psychiatrist for seven years. I became the full-time manager of our household, while learning to be more humble in the process. By the way, I am still a work in progress on being more humble, ha ha! I thank God that Mom had trained me well on how to shop for groceries and keep an eye out for bargains, and I must admit that I am pretty good at it too!

I am very proud of Lynn and what I know about her service as a psychiatrist. She was admired and highly respected by patients, staff, and colleagues alike. Psychiatry was indeed her calling and her ministry and brought purpose and meaning to her life. One of her colleagues, who was also a councilman, nominated Lynn for Woman of the Year in Fresno, an honor she truly deserved.

Lynn found a deep meaning in her professional life as a psychiatrist and became known as one of the top doctors at her hospital. We both believed that she would continue working in this fashion for a many more years, but that was not to be the case. Over a few short months her career came to a screeching halt.

MY SECOND ACT

The Call of the...Northeast?

Through the years, I began to nourish the desire to someday return to the east coast to live out my "golden years." I had conflicting feelings because I knew deep down in my heart that you can never really go back. My New York personality never did fit in with the West Coast mindset. Somebody once told me the saying that New Yorkers stab you in the front and Californians stab you in the back. I must admit that the longer I lived in central California, the less I enjoyed it, and the more I missed my east coast roots. I was oblivious to the fact that we had spent well over 30 years in this town and had established wide and deep roots and connections and built our professional careers here. I was concerned about the fact that we were both aging day by day (isn't everybody?) and not much else. Then came the day about six years ago when my son-in-law announced he was being recruited by a successful financial advisor/wealth manager from a firm in the northeast. Even though my daughter was raised in California, she has always been an East Coast kind of girl. We would often go to New York for our summer trips and vacations, and sometimes at Christmas. He subsequently accepted the position, and in short order, Lynn and I were there at the airport waving goodbye to them.

CHAPTER 17

So, there we were, empty nesters in central California. Why it seemed like just yesterday we were young parents raising our three children. Our son was in LA and our daughter and her young family in the northeast. It was at that point that the wheels in my mind began slowly turning. They had settled in the Philadelphia area not far from my Yonkers roots. Lynn and I began to pray and discuss what our future might look like. My love and devotion for my daughter were simply so strong that I knew in my heart I had to be near her and the grandkids. My heart's desire was to continue my legacy as the generational change agent and become the grandfather I never had. Lynn and I had been doing this as parents over the years. Now my family deserved my very best and with the remaining time I would be blessed to live in this earthly body. It energized me when I would fantasize about what a new start in life in the northeast would look like.

What I failed to realize about Lynn is that change in general is much more difficult for her. Looking back, I was too busy planning to stop and listen. After all, Lynn has always been quite sentimental and nostalgic, and I never fathomed she might feel differently. We even prayed to come into agreement about our future move. To my recollection, both of us were feeling that God was in the plans for us to relocate to the northeast. One of her prayer partners had envisioned a beautiful house on a hill which could serve as a joint ministry center. My dream was to get into active Papa mode. I envisioned that Lynn and I would bond more deeply with our daughter, son-in-law, and young grandchildren, and that all of us would grow older and live happily ever after.

The Air of Change

We began to actively look for a place to live in the northeast while making our Central Valley home ready for inspection and sale as an honest home. This home was a large, spacious, and beautiful home full of light and love. At its peak, we had six people living there, and there were cherished memories everywhere in the house. As the kids left, it felt to me like some of those memories left also. Suddenly, it was just the two of us living in that huge house. I truly felt that a house this size was meant for a family, not just two people. I could sense that change was in the air when seemingly out of nowhere, the bottom dropped out.

CHAPTER 17

Once a Diagnostic Radiologist, Always a Diagnostic Radiologist

We were all involved in the midst of the planning phase, then one day in February 2021, quite unexpectedly, Lynn developed a very unusual lower back pain that would come and go, sometimes migrating to either or both hips. The MRI of her lower back was negative, and the physical medicine doctor thought she was having muscle spasms. He gave her trigger point injections bringing some relief. Different symptoms developed about a month later when she started to get neck and upper back pain. The doctor was perplexed but proceeded with more injections. Then came the ominous symptoms of pain and numbness starting to affect both arms as well as cold sensations in both hands. An MRI of her neck and cervical spine was finally obtained in May just to be sure that there were no serious underlying spinal problems. I have to say it has been a mixed blessing for me to be a diagnostic radiologist. I performed objectively at a high-level when I interpreted studies of all the different patients, I had the privilege to investigate. When it came to functioning as a doctor with my own family members, it was quite another story. One can easily lose objectivity.

After her exam, I obtained the DVD of her MRI. The

radiologist who interpreted her exam would not see it until the following day. I was the first doctor to look at the MRI and begin to diagnose her situation. I remember sitting at my desktop computer and popping the CD in, fully expecting (and hoping) to see a normal study. Much to my shock and dismay it was a very abnormal study. My jaw dropped and I blurted out an expletive as I tried to disprove the bad findings and wish it normal. Try as I might, I could not make the swelling in her spinal cord disappear. Glaring right at me was a dangerous situation and it felt like I was looking down the barrel of a gun. There was a very severe narrowing in her upper cervical spine that compressed her spinal cord. This dangerous medical situation could have led to Lynn being paralyzed and she needed urgent neurosurgical help before it became a true neurosurgical emergency.

A Gradual Worsening

I struggled for words as I relayed to Lynn just how bad her situation was. Initially, she took the news like it was no big deal. She was initially calm and composed. I believe that the defense mechanism of denial can be helpful early on. Refusing to acknowledge the disturbing aspects of one's external reality or of ongoing internal events can initially

CHAPTER 17

be helpful to avoid falling into the great chasm of pain and fear. However, that can only last so long and reality eventually catches up with you. Later, she was distraught, and we prayed together. I pledged my undying support, no matter what. The following day I went into MD mode and reached out to two of my most revered neuroradiology professors at my previous university. I emailed each one independently and posed the following question. If either they or a family member had a similar situation with their cervical spine, where would they go to get the best care available? Amazingly, each promptly replied and recommended the same neurosurgeon at their university. Lynn's symptoms were gradually worsening but somehow with God's help I was able to arrange two separate neurosurgical consultations for the same day and on very short notice. One of these was a virtual meeting with the university neurosurgeon; the other was in person with a colleague of mine at my hospital. This fellow is a fine physician and was both honest and transparent. He was willing to do the operation along with his partner, but at their facility they just didn't do many operations with this level of complexity. When I asked him the critical question, "if you had to have this type of operation, where would you go?" His response intersected with the two previous professors. I firmly believe that God certainly was in the details.

Four weeks later Lynn had a three-level laminectomy along with fusion of her cervical spine. On a technical level, the operation was a huge success. We had both hoped and prayed for a total cure, however, neither of us was prepared for what was to follow over the next several months.

I learned first-hand about deepening my sacrificial love. Over the short haul I learned to function as a nurse with Lynn. Her whole world had been shocked and rocked, body, mind, and spirit. As a result, she became more anxious, depressed, and dependent. It was quite difficult for me to put myself in her shoes. I know in my heart I did the very best that I could, but even with that, I was also struggling. Her physical symptoms of pain and soreness with muscle spasms and cold sensations in her hands continued. For Lynn to continue working as a psychiatrist full time, or even part time, was totally out of the question in the immediate future. Enter another big stressor—forced retirement when she wasn't anywhere near ready. Just getting up in the morning and making it through the day was about all she could handle for the time being.

Rest, Recuperation; Rest, Delay

The neurosurgeon told us that she would need about two months to recover from the surgery. After that, she would

CHAPTER 17

be cleared to move to the East Coast. While that was probably true from a surgical point of view, it turned out that proclamation was overly optimistic. As time dragged on, it became apparent that there may be some residual damage to her spinal cord that just might not return. I believed in my heart that I was doing the right thing by delaying our move for a couple of more months until October. My rationale was that a couple of additional months of rest and recuperation would be sufficient to help Lynn regain the energy for the move. We had bought the home in the Philadelphia area a few months before and were still in the process of selling our current home. I was just itching to leave California and begin the new chapters of our lives on the east coast. I just didn't imagine how homesick Lynn would become when we finally did make the move. Looking back on that time, maybe I just didn't want to acknowledge this possibility.

The summer of 2021 was a hot one for the housing market. That, coupled with Lynn's unexpected surgery, helped create a buying frenzy in us. While we and our daughter had looked at several homes in the previous months, we ended up buying our east coast home based solely on photos, videos, and recommendations. On paper, that home checked all the boxes on our list. I learned at least one valuable lesson through this difficult time—never buy a home sight unseen. It is also best to explore whatever problems there are and get accurate estimates on the cost of fixing or replacing. I also determined that it's best to deal with one major issue at a time. And I truly wished I had stopped and listened more carefully to what was going on inside of Lynn. She just wasn't ready to move.

Let the Buyer Beware

So that fall we moved, locked, stock, and barrel with all our stuff (and a lot of junk) to our new east coast home. Almost from the get-go, we reaped the consequences of buying a home with an antiquated septic system that had failed inspection. We were naïve and accepted the seller's compensation towards repair or replacement of that system. We all assumed that the sum of money would cover most of the cost. What do they say about the word assume? After our home closed, one septic system company told us that we had to accept the fact that our septic system was failing. We were told there were no other options, and their recommendation was to obtain low flow toilets. With a firm belief that there are always solutions, a few months later I hired a prominent soil scientist. After a thorough investigation, he determined that we had only one viable option, a micro drip filtration system.

CHAPTER 17

The compensation that we had received from the seller only served as a small down payment and in reality, was a small fraction of the true cost. After a lot of blood, sweat, and tears, I've learned to be more discerning about what I'm actually getting into before jumping in head long. At least I'm not too old to still learn from mistakes.

Much Harder Than We Anticipated

On a different note, I had adapted to the temperate climate of the northeast like a fish to water. It reminded me of my younger days back in New York. The weather was alive, varying greatly from day to day. It can be sunny and beautiful in the morning, then in the afternoon one might hear thunder and see storm clouds off in the distance. Soon the sky darkens and here comes a wonderful thunderstorm. For Lynn, it was just the opposite. That fall and winter revealed that she had seasonal affective disorder. The cold intensified her symptoms, as well as pain and coldness in her body. Her physical and emotional symptoms worsened to such a degree that we needed to re-examine our current situation. My dream of living out our days as one big happy family with Lynn and me being model grandparents was fading away. It was quite difficult for Lynn to get out of bed in the morning, let alone participate in settling our new home. I immersed myself in decluttering and hired various professional organizers. This greatly helped potentiate what I could do in a few selected dedicated hours. I soon discovered that we had packed and shipped *all* our belongings, including old professional books, and many items we did not need or would ever use. I became angry and frustrated and anxious as I struggled to quell the fire inside of me. I was angry with both of us for not having adequately prepared to move. Failure to do this wasted several thousand dollars which could have been put to much better use. Please don't make the same mistakes that we did. Make sure you declutter before you move, and that the things that you take with you, you truly love and will use. It sure can save a lot of time, aggravation, and money.

    Neither of us are what you might call typical homeowners. I envy the folks who enjoy doing projects around their home, however that is not our cup of tea. I will participate in home organization provided I have an incentive such as a professional organizer to act as a catalyst. Neither of us was prepared for maintaining a home on an acre of land with a septic system, well, and pool at this phase of our lives. True that they were first world or champagne problems. They were still very real, not exactly the kind of challenges that I ever expected to face

CHAPTER 17

while in retirement. Looking back on our lives, each of us were highly skilled and respected professionals, and there's only so much that one can do during the day and with one's life. As time went on, Lynn began to feel better, and even was hinting about returning to her career, which had given her so much purpose and meaning. For now, my purpose and meaning were tied up in household duties and helping care for our precious grandchildren.

CHAPTER 18
DASHED DREAMS OF HAPPILY-EVER-AFTER

Our first winter back in the northeast after over 40 years in sunny California shocked us into reality. As I mentioned, Lynn continued to suffer. The cold began to affect my knee joints so badly that at times I crawled up the stairs. Later, I learned that I have degenerative joint disease in both of my knees. Both of us were raised to believe that when the going gets tough, the tough get going. Soon we experienced our first snowfall of the season. We joined forces and shoveled the snow off our driveway. What a novelty to get to shovel snow again after a 45-year break! That cold winter proved to be the last season of life for our Maltese dog, Teddy. He had a colorful life being a small dog with a big attitude. He left his mark in our quiet rural neighborhood after nipping a young neighbor boy on the hand. He always left an impression. He remained dedicated to me until the very end. When it came time to let him go, I asked the vet and his assistant if they could

CHAPTER 18

let me go with him; they respectively declined. Teddy was now free from all his pain and suffering–ours on the other hand, remained and worsened.

Little by little, I felt my dream of living happily ever after on the east coast as doting grandparents continue to slip away. Both of us were in pain and unhappy, but for different reasons. Lynn had the aftermath of the trauma of surgery, along with residual spinal cord damage. Add to that forced retirement, moving to a new location, and leaving many cherished friends and acquaintances. It became too much for her to bear. My usual way of life involved serving others, and getting things accomplished. It was it a big shock for me to discover that my best plans and intentions had failed. I allowed anger, sadness, and resentment to fill my mind and heart and for a long time felt like I was in this battle alone. I really thought God had forgotten about me. Where were you God when I needed you? And where are you now?

Following the Sun

Lynn and I decided to take frequent trips back to California. It was slowly becoming clear to me that Lynn was much more alive and happier when we were back in our familiar town. Over time it became clear to me that Lynn desired to have a second home in the central valley. It was also evident that our daughter and son supported this, as they also have many fond memories and connections there; plus, my son-in-law's family lives there. An additional bonus was our son Sammy lived in downtown LA, certainly within driving distance. I slowly began to entertain the idea. I realized my best friend Pastor Doug, Warrior Fitness, my fishing buddy, and professional fishing guide for the San Joaquin River remained in Fresno, along with our favorite restaurants, other friends and acquaintances. Our beloved religious community was there as well. But somehow it seemed I needed further confirmation.

Lynn and I went to Bonita Springs on the Florida gulf coast the following January to escape the cold and get some Florida sunshine. This was shortly after hurricane Ian wreaked its havoc on the southwest coast of Florida. Just seeing the massive destruction around Fort Meyers beach and hearing stories of beach homes being carried out to sea from the 15-foot storm surge made my problems pale in comparison. That was my last-ditch effort in hopes that we might be like other snowbirds and have our winter home in Florida. But that was not to be. A couple of unusual events occurred within the last few days of our trip. Lynn tripped and fell, breaking her shoulder. I

CHAPTER 18

developed wheezing and was prescribed prednisone for suspected reactive airways disease. Upon returning home it worsened into pneumonia. I interpret these two events almost as a warning from God about getting our second home in Florida.

Learning to Let God Lead

Somehow through this, I began to incorporate this notion to let God direct our paths and trust in Him to lead us as we seek Him through prayer. How you view and respond to failure in life, namely your attitude, will define your progress. I love one of Winston Churchill's most famous quotes, "Never give in." I have not arrived at the place where I can completely relax and rest, but I am slowly learning to let God guide me more and more in every situation according to His purposes. As a result, I am trusting Him more and more for the outcome. Pastor Doug often uses the phrase "to bring honor and glory to God in all that comes across my path today." I am working on that.

CHAPTER 19
MY ACCORDIAN LIFE

When people ask me how I chose the accordion as a musical instrument to play, I tell them that the accordion actually hand-picked me. One spring day, when I was about 9 or 10, I was playing with my brothers and sister in the playroom of our house. Suddenly a knock at our front door, and next thing I know Mom is chatting with this dapper fellow, who looked like a traveling salesman. He introduced himself to Mom and asked her if anybody in our house would like to learn to play the piano, the violin, or the accordion. Mom instantly narrowed it down to a choice of one, spouting out the question, "Who wants to learn the accordion?" My knee-jerk reflex was to immediately volunteer as there seemed to be no time to think about it. What if one of my siblings volunteered before me? I might not get the opportunity. Why not take the chance? Maybe I would learn something. That well-dressed Jewish fellow turned out to be a musical genius

CHAPTER 19

who was working hard to support his wife and children by teaching music lessons and instruments.

For the first couple of years of lessons he would come to our house. I started out with this small red accordion, and oh how I loved that accordion. He helped me navigate through the entire Palmer Hughes accordion course. As it turned out, I had a special gift of learning music and play the accordion. Music became a great outlet for me, especially with my Polish heritage. My favorite kind of music became polkas and other folk songs, as well as contemporary songs. I particularly enjoyed playing for Mom and Dad and at family gatherings and parties. Once I performed for some New York socialites at a swank Halloween party on the upper east side. A fellow accordion student and I auditioned for the Ted Mack Amateur Hour and although we didn't make the cut, the experience was enjoyable and memorable. During the five years I was with my instructor, I also participated in the American Accordionists Association National Championship Contest around age 15. I ranked fourth in the New York State Accordion Championship Contest, narrowly missing the third-place trophy; nevertheless, I was delighted with my progress.

MY ACCORDIAN LIFE

A Return to My Music

In college I had progressively less time to devote to practicing and playing the accordion. By then I had acquired a beautiful black Titano120 bass instrument that my parents had bought for me, and to this day, I still enjoy playing it. I ventured on to pursue my career in medicine and radiology, rarely picking up the accordion to play for nearly 40 years. Soon after I retired at age 60, I developed a yearning in my heart to take up the accordion once again. I began thinking about resuming accordion lessons in order to kick it up a notch and take my skills to the next level. This was one of the gifts I gave myself as I embarked on my second half. The fellow who tuned our parlor grand piano was at the house one day, and as an accomplished musician himself was very connected to musicians in the community. I asked him if he knew a good accordionist I could take lessons from. He told me he had just the guy for me. One of his oldest friends and acquaintances was this old Italian master jazz accordionist. A week or two later I learned that this fellow would be performing at one of our favorite Italian restaurants. Between numbers, I walked up to him and introduced myself stating that I wanted to take music lessons from him. Years later, he retold the story about our meeting, and he simply thought

CHAPTER 19

I was giving him a line of bull, and that I never would follow through, just like many people had done before in his life. But this time I proved him wrong.

My new accordion teacher was tough and that's even with him having mellowed some over the years. He once told me a story that back in the day whenever his accordion student hadn't practiced for the week, he would have that child pack up the accordion and go home, telling his mother don't bother coming back until he had practiced. He gave me weekly assignments that really helped me raise my level of proficiency. He hand wrote some of the songs and gave me jazzed up additions of other songs. In his prime, he was probably one of the best jazz accordionists in the country, and I was honing my skills learning from a true master. I was very blessed to have had him as my mentor for approximately five years. Once I matriculated, I would join his group of students once a month when we would get together at either a retirement home or assisted living facility. Each student would perform a couple of songs for the residents in those facilities. What a joy it was to see how happy those folks were as they watched us perform. That experience alone was worth every single moment of practice. As my mentor declined in health, we took advantage of opportunities to socialize with him and his wife. On one memorable occasion we treated them to see Johnny Mathis perform his Christmas show in Fresno. As it turns out our accordion teacher knew Johnny's drummer, so at the end we got to go backstage and meet Johnny in person. As he was declining in health, he told me that when he passed away one of his wishes was for me to play the song, "My One and Only Love" at his memorial service. I was honored to play that slow and jazzy song, trying my best to emulate the music of John Coltrane and Johnny Hartman's version.

The Song of Life—Get Up and Dance

In many ways I've grown to view my life as a metaphor for playing the accordion. As I would pull out the bellows, the air is drawn in, like life expanding with joy, contentment, wonderful times, and full family experiences. This is indeed a time to be grateful to God for the abundance of life and all its blessings. As the air is expelled and the bellows contract, these are the hard times. Various emotions such as fear, anger, sadness, and even death, come into the picture. I believe it's best to enjoy the music while the bellows are moving. Both movements—the good times and the bad times—are necessary to complete the entire song of life. As long as you have breath, keep on playing and don't get stuck in either position. If you're not already there, get on the dance floor and dance.

CHAPTER 20
LOSS, LESSONS LEARNED, AND LEGACY

Writing and revising this book over the last several months has been an emotional roller coaster for me. My goal has been to showcase where God has brought me to this point. During this process, I learned the truth that I wasn't done grieving over the loss of David. Maybe I never will. Through my own sadness I have come to a more peaceful place of acceptance. I'm reminded of the poem "Footprints in the Sand," where the author asks God, why, during the most trying periods of his life, were there only one set of footprints in the sand. God replied, that was when He carried that man.

I learned much more about myself during this journey. For one thing, my initial choice to become a psychiatrist had as its root cause my deep unconscious desire to heal myself and my family. How liberating it was to have that burden lifted off my shoulders! I feel that God was right beside me as I discovered the field of diagnostic radiology. The typical radiologist is primarily an investigative individual who is quite inquisitive and curious with an aptitude for problem solving. Imaging has always intrigued me, and I was equipped with a dogged determination to arrive at an accurate diagnosis. God, however, directed Lynn to become a psychiatrist, and I have a vicariously enjoyed bits and pieces of that field as seen through her eyes.

The tools I received through my life journey are priceless, but they did not come without a huge cost. It is apparent to me that suffering can lead to a person becoming bitter or better, or maybe even a combination. That's where the Jesus factor became a game changer for me. At this stage in my life my faith in God is greater than it has ever been before. Reviewing my life has brought me to the foot of the cross. Jesus became God/man for us. He lived a human life, experienced and felt everything, just like all of us. He willingly accepted his fate to die on the cross for all our sins. Yet He emerged victorious. No matter how difficult our journey, Christ leads us to the end of the road and life eternal. We all have free access to a right relationship with Him by believing and accepting Him into our hearts.

Through my relationship with God, I am learning to truly love myself, Lynn, family, and others more unconditionally. Several months ago, we had our 40th wedding

CHAPTER 20

anniversary and recently I reached a milestone birthday becoming age 70. Now that both of our parents are gone, we are the elders in our family. What kind of legacy will each of us leave? For that matter, how many more productive years are left? I am grateful not to know the answer to that question as only God knows.

Pastor Doug has marveled at how God miraculously has come along side Lynn and me to maintain our marriage. After going through a heartbreaking situation with a medically fragile child, losing that child, causes many marriages to end, either in separation or divorce. God has seen us through those times. True love involves sacrifice and serving one another, even when it may not be returned in kind. Jesus was the ultimate servant who constantly walked in love and forgiveness. While serving others, it is very important to take care of your own desires, wants and needs in the process.

Recently, becoming predominantly alcohol free has been a major game changer for me. Some of the many benefits I have gained is being much more awake alive, and in tune during the day, with a clearer mind, and better control of my emotions. My physical health has improved as has my quality of sleep no more lousy hangovers. My vacation from alcohol is being nourished by my participation in a program called This Naked Mind, and offshoots of this program. This is an innovative, non-judgmental program which was started by Annie Grace. It has been sobering to explore the harmful and toxic effects of alcohol. My plan is to carry that forward, one day at a time. There are several great programs to support people through recovery such as Alcoholics Anonymous and in the Christian churches, Celebrate Recovery. Alcohol remains a highly addictive substance deeply woven into our culture, but with God's help along with accountability groups, that foe can be defeated.

It is of utmost importance that I remind myself that I am worthy to love and be loved. Recently I have also prayed almost every morning, making prayer my first morning ritual. I use this helpful acronym that I learned many years ago. It is ACTS; that stands for Adoration, Confession, Thanksgiving, and Supplication. Having daily gratitude has become very important. I currently find great comfort and wisdom in the book of Psalms. I believe that God enjoys it when you take time to listen to His voice in your heart.

One thing that remains hard for me to do is to devote time to recreational activities. I personally enjoy working out with a group called Warrior Fitness and the fellow who runs it was trained as a Navy seal, and it is indeed a para-military workout. This culture maintains a warrior

CHAPTER 20

spirit which prevails in the face of adversity. The greater the struggle, the greater the ultimate victory. I also enjoy fishing, playing the accordion, and having special dinners with Lynn and family.

My ultimate goal is to leave a legacy of love when my time comes. I believe that a life well lived includes giving of your time, talent, and treasure. To whom much is given, much is required, and it remains of paramount importance to nurture your relationships. The experience of writing my life's story will be worth it if my journey helps any of you, my readers. May you live your life well, full of purpose, and meaning. Onward and upward!

www.ingramcontent.com/pod-product-compliance
Lightning Source LLC
Chambersburg PA
CBHW050527170426
43201CB00013B/2114